Arthur Crump

A Practical Treatise on Banking, Currency and the Exchanges

Arthur Crump

A Practical Treatise on Banking, Currency and the Exchanges

ISBN/EAN: 9783742807045

Manufactured in Europe, USA, Canada, Australia, Japa

Cover: Foto ©knipser5 / pixelio.de

Manufactured and distributed by brebook publishing software
(www.brebook.com)

Arthur Crump

A Practical Treatise on Banking, Currency and the Exchanges

A PRACTICAL TREATISE

ON

BANKING, CURRENCY, AND

THE EXCHANGES

BY

ARTHUR CRUMP

BANK MANAGER

FORMERLY OF THE BANK OF ENGLAND

LONDON

LONGMANS, GREEN, AND CO.

1866

PREFACE.

—◦—

'Une science ne fait de véritables progrès que lorsqu'on est parvenu à bien déterminer le champ où peuvent s'étendre ses recherches et l'objet qu'elles doivent se proposer; autrement on saisit çà et là un petit nombre de vérités sans en connaître la liaison, et beaucoup d'erreurs sans en pouvoir découvrir la fausseté.'*

I VENTURE to submit the present volume for the approval of the public, in the hope that its perusal—more especially by the rising members of the profession, whose daily occupation is practical banking—may awaken a livelier interest in, and lead to a more general study of these subjects; and it will, I trust, not prove uninstrumental in inducing them to bring what experience they may have had to assist in the discussion

* Traité d'Économie Politique, par Jean-Baptiste Say.

of any measures of banking reform that may be
proposed from time to time.

It would seem not only desirable but necessary
that when suggestions are thrown out for the
improvement of methods and systems, practical
bankers should be the recognised authorities, by
virtue of their closer acquaintance with the
practice of their craft.

The study of the theory and practice of banking
no doubt suffers considerable neglect by reason
of there being no special qualifications demanded
of those who are elected into the service of
banking institutions. A student seldom takes a
deep interest in any subject until he has removed
much of that elementary matter which forms the
exterior crust of all sciences, and which requires
diligent application to succeed in penetrating;
after which the interest becomes more and more
engaged.

The career of a banker's clerk for the first few

years is comparatively a waste of time, so far as
any progress in the science of his profession is
concerned. There can be no reasons given why
men should not be compelled to pass a commercial
examination previous to engaging in business of
any kind—business that cannot be termed exactly
trade—any more than for medicine or the army;
and if such a system were introduced, there can be
little doubt that in many instances men would be
induced to continue the study of financial and
banking questions, and thereby materially assist
in elucidating some of the points which are so
frequently brought forward for discussion, and let
drop again without any satisfactory solution
having been arrived at. We see occasionally
brilliant attacks made upon this or that part of
our commercial machinery, as it proves unequal
to the strain; but from the intricacy and wide
spread of all the practical details, which must be
thoroughly examined before any reform of one

part can be carried through without injury to another, it is necessary that the attention of those who are daily in the habit of practically dealing with such matters, should be aroused to consider and deliberate upon any proposed change, so that the persons whose habits of thought lie in the groove in which we require amelioration, should be brought to interest themselves more, and assist in perfecting the means at our disposal.

The present volume will be found to contain information gathered from various sources, the advantage of which in a *condensed* form has occurred to me during my banking career, and I trust, beyond being useful so far as it goes, it will stimulate to further research.

If the perusal of this humble effort may lead my fellow-workers to profit—however little—by what they may glean here, and push on farther into the depths of the subjects which will yet be productive of a rich store, I shall consider myself rewarded in the thought that I have aroused some attention to questions which, as a rule, are much neglected by the rising members of the banking profession.

I must, in conclusion, offer my sincere thanks to my friend Mr. John Douglas Farrell, of the Bank of England, for his valuable advice and assistance during the compilation of this volume, more especially with reference to the chapter on ' Notes.'

A. C.

CONTENTS.

CHAPTER V.

CHAPTER VI.

CHAPTER VII.

CHAPTER VIII.

CHAPTER IX.

CHAPTER X.

CHAPTER XI.

BANKING

CHAPTER I.

PART I.

THE ORIGIN AND USES OF BANKS.

THE WORD 'BANK' is derived from the Italian
word 'banco,' a bench, which was erected in the
market-place, where it was customary to exchange
money. The Lombard Jews were the first to
practise this system, the first bench having been
established in Italy A.D. 808. Some authorities
assert that the Lombard merchants commenced
the business of money-dealing—employing bills of
exchange as remittances—about the beginning of
the thirteenth century; and that such a practice
was also known in the south of France about the
same period. Other authorities give these benches
the name of *cambii*, informing us that they were

B

placed before the church doors for the purpose
of exchanging the money of foreigners. These
money-changers obtained the names of Lombards,
or Cahoursini, the latter from a celebrated money-
changer who flourished in the south of France.
The Lombards spread themselves far and wide,
finding their trade very profitable, and soon became established in every country. The tendency
to imposition caused a supervision by the magistrates to be brought about, who obliged the
bankers to deposit a certain sum as a guarantee
for their good faith. Among other countries, these
Jews found their way to England, and carried on
their trade in the city of London; the street
which they selected for their operations having
borne the name of Lombard Street ever since,
where some of the principal banks in London still
carry on their business. These Lombard merchants were believed in England to have been
natives of one of the four republics of Genoa,
Lucca, Florence, or Venice,* and were supposed
to have been sent to England by Pope Gregory
IX. to provide convents and other societies with
money; it having been made known that they

* Anderson 'On Commerce.'

were unable to pay the 'tenths,' which were rigorously enforced that year, 13 Henry III., 1229. The Lombard Jews were notorious for their usurious transactions, and they carried them to such an extent that they were expelled from the country in the reign of Queen Elizabeth.

When these Jews failed in Lombardy, their benches were broken by the populace, and hence our word *bankrupt*.

We find that 'argentaria' was the ancient Latin name for a bank or money-changer's shop, and that the banker or money-changer was called 'argentarius.' As these Lombard Jews came into such disrepute for their usurious dealings, they subsequently changed their name for 'cambiator' or 'cambitor,' meaning an exchanger. We learn that Philip the Fair formed these money-dealers into a corporation, and security was demanded by James II. of Arragon, previous to their commencing business, according to the statutes of Marseilles. Bills of exchange are said to have originated with these cambitores. Persons about to travel, instead of encumbering themselves with coin, applied to a cambitor and received in exchange for their specie a bill of exchange drawn upon another cambitor, as near as possible to the place where they were going. These letters were called *literæ cambitoriæ*. Accurate information about the mode in which such documents were drawn is impossible to obtain. Some have recorded that these bills were drawn payable to a certain person; others assert that they were payable to bearer, and circulated from one to the other like our bank-notes. It is tolerably certain, however, that the Jews would pursue a system which conduced more to their own advantage than that of the public.

About the middle of the twelfth century it became evident, as the advantage of coined money was gradually acknowledged, that there must be some controlling power, some corporation of men who would undertake to keep the coins — that were to bear the royal stamp — up to a certain standard of value; as, independently of the 'sweating'*—which invention we may place to the credit of the ingenuity of the Lombard merchants—all coins will, by wear or abrasion, become thinner, and consequently less valuable; and it is of the last importance, not only for the credit

* A term given to various processes invented by the Jews for obtaining a small quantity of gold from each sovereign, or other gold coin, without the loss being perceptible.

of a country, but for the easier regulation of commercial transactions, that the metallic currency be kept up to the standard. Much unnecessary trouble and annoyance has been caused by a disregard of the coinage being kept up to the standard of value originally fixed upon. England has, at more than one period of her history, suffered the most humiliating degradation by the neglect not only to keep her coinage up to the standard, but to insure the employment of persons to superintend the operations of the mint, who were endowed with moral rectitude, and whose integrity could not be purchased by the state. Large sums were obtained for royal purposes in the reign of Henry VIII. by falsifying the silver standard; and it fell to the lot of a woman, in the person of Queen Elizabeth, together with her advisers, to stamp the debased coins with their real value. These practices, however, we shall have occasion to investigate further, in a subsequent chapter.

The gradual merging of the business of a goldsmith into a bank appears to have been the way in which banking, as we now understand the term, was introduced into England; and it was not until long after the establishment of banks in other countries—for State purposes, the regulation

of the coinage, &c.—that any large or similar institution sprang into existence in England. We
hereto annex a table of the principal banks, as
they were established in different parts of the
world, in chronological order.

The most important banks that had been established up to the year 1791 are the following:—

		A.D.
Bank of Venice . .	established	1171
„ Geneva . .	„	1345
„ Barcelona . .	„	1401
„ Genoa . .	„	1407
„ Amsterdam .	„	1609
„ Hamburg . .	„	1619
„ Rotterdam . .	„	1635
„ Stockholm . .	„	1688
„ England . .	„	1691
„ Scotland . .	„	1695
„ France . .	„	1716
„ Copenhagen .	„	1736
„ Berlin . .	„	1765
Caisse d'Escompte, France .	„	1776
Bank of Ireland . .	„	1783
„ St. Petersburg .	„	1786
Bank in the East Indies .	„	1787
„ North America .	„	1791

Branch banks were commenced in England in
the year 1828.

Between the dates of the establishment of the
bank at Rotterdam and that at Stockholm, Mr.
Francis Child started a bank on the eastern side

of Temple Bar, London. He had for many years previously adopted the armorial bearings of the Lombards, and pursued the respectable vocation of a goldsmith, or what we understand to be a pawnbroker. This business he merged into a banking-house, which is still in existence. The banking firm of Child & Co. still carries on business under the same name; and as a proof of how people will adhere to ancient customs, it is only within the last few years that *printed* cheques have been in use in that establishment. The banking-house of Child & Co. was established in 1663, Hoare & Co. about 1675, and Snow & Co. 1680; this last having had thirteen years' experience before the Bank of England was established. The Bank of Scotland was established one year later, and it was not till 1783 that the Bank of Ireland commenced operations at St. Mary's Abbey, Dublin.

Concerning the invention of Venetian banks, there appear to be several opinions. Some say the first was contrived in 1150, others 1157. There was no doubt a sort of bank established at one or other of these dates for the purpose of assisting in arranging a loan for the Venetians, and that this institution was called the 'Chamber of Loans;' but the Bank of Venice was not founded till 1171.

There can be little doubt that the word 'banking' was a term originally applied to the business of those persons whose chief trade was to lend out their *own* money, and that the back-bone of their establishments did not consist of the money of other people, which was intrusted to them in the form of deposits. In this opinion most writers appear to agree. That such a business would develop itself into what we find in modern institutions is only natural; as simply time would be required to prove that other people's money could be employed by the banker to the advantage of both himself and the depositor.

When the practice of lending money at interest was originated is not known, but from the progress made in other sciences — without it being necessary to ascertain the date — we may safely presume that such a practice was adopted from the earliest times.

We learn that money-lending was carried on very extensively after the return from the captivity; that the poor obtained money from the rich by mortgaging their lands, houses, &c.

The parable of the talents distinctly indicates

that money, as the representative of capital, was not to be allowed to lie idle.

We find also that the Athenians, as early as B.C. 146, converted their temples into banks of deposit, from which they were in the habit of lending to the public at interest.

Mr. Macleod tells us in his first volume of 'The Theory and Practice of Banking,' that the business of banking at Athens was in full vigour in the time of Demosthenes, and that the rate of interest was left absolutely free by Solon. Solon also had the extreme good sense, even at that early period, to see the absurdity of imprisonment for debt, and took away the right. Further on he tells us that 'the first mention of banking at Rome is in the year B.C. 352, when the Plebeians were in deep distress, and had to borrow money from new creditors to pay off the principal and interest of their old debts, and so got deeper and deeper into debt.' 'Another class of bankers, who were a permanent institution, were named *mensularii* or *numularii*, who both acted for the State, and also received the deposits of private individuals. They were also authorised by the State to act as exchangers, and give Roman coins for foreign ones at a fixed rate of exchange.

Those who were entirely private bankers were
called *argentarii*. These private bankers trans-
acted their business very much as many modern
ones do; they kept their customers' accounts, and
they introduced one of the greatest conveniences
in the system of banking, viz. making payments
by means of cheques. A cheque was called
attributio or *prescriptio*. They also made use of
promissory notes.'

The progress, however, in the science of banking
attained to but a feeble growth either among the
Greeks or Romans, and it was left to countries
whose commercial prosperity has reached that of
England or France, to push to their present perfection the banking facilities which are now afforded
to those engaged in commerce, &c.

The bank next in European importance to the
one established by the magistrates at Barcelona in
1401 was the Bank of St. George at Genoa, which,
like the Bank of England, came into existence
through the necessities of the State—large sums
of money having been borrowed from the citizens
from time to time, the interest of which was paid
out of the revenue. It became at length too
extensive an affair to be properly conducted unless
under the management of an efficiently organised

administration; which having been established, the creditors' claims were consolidated to form a capital, with which the Bank of St. George commenced its career. The Austrians pillaged the Bank of St. George in 1746, from which it never recovered.

The Bank of Amsterdam was established in 1609, adopting the same course as the Venetians —receiving the clipped and worn coins at a value equal to their weight in bullion, with the deduction for management and the expenses of recoinage. This Bank of Amsterdam appears to have set an example worthy of all praise, for it received the coins of *all* nations for the purpose of encouraging the bullion trade. The bank, by this means, prevented for the time the wear and tear of the coins by keeping them in their vaults, whilst the bank receipts circulated as notes, giving the bank the right to dispose of the bullion if not redeemed after a certain period of time had elapsed.

The citizens of Hamburg established a bank ten years later. It granted loans upon the security of precious stones among other peculiarities, and has even now a reputation attaching to it of adhering to antiquated and cumbrous systems, which one would hardly expect in a city which has reached

that high degree of commercial importance which
Hamburg may be said justly to have attained.

PART II.

In reviewing the progress made by banks, as
they were established in different parts of the
world, we must of necessity keep before us the
commercial standing of the countries in which
these banks were created. Those nations which,
from their geographical position, are shut out of
the principal lines of commercial traffic, will be
less likely to advance in that direction in which
the facilities of banking are suggested by necessity
—although commerce (from the Latin *commutatio
mercium*) has existed since one commodity was
exchanged for another, and, as Mr. M'Culloch
says, 'is coeval with the first dawn of civilisation.'
The perfection of our present system of banking—
which in many respects is yet far from *quite* perfect
—could never have been brought about in the
absence of that enormous trade, and the consequent
necessity for economy of time and means, which
the existing inhabitants of Great Britain have lived
to see. It is not our intention to introduce the

figures by which England has for so long a period
dwarfed the efforts of every other country, in
respect of either exports or imports. It is simply
our intention to show that banking, as a great part
of the machinery by which commercial transactions
are conducted, could only have been advanced to
its present state of perfection by the strain which
has been constantly brought to bear upon old and
cumbrous systems, until they have been gradually
swept away by the genius and labour of a hard-
working, practical, and enlightened people, whose
mercantile prosperity has caused them to seek by
degrees for improved methods.

No definite records having been handed down
to us which throw any light upon the question as
to whether written documents were used or not,
we may presume that the commerce which is said
to have flourished in Arabia, Egypt, and among
the Phœnicians, in the earliest ages, was but a
simple system of barter. Later on, we find that
commercial relations existed A.D. 1241, by a
confederation of maritime cities over the continent
of Europe. The enterprise of the Portuguese and
Dutch, added to the discoveries of Columbus, considerably enlarged the sphere of commerce; and
this, we are informed, induced England to engage

extensively in its pursuit. England's first commercial treaty was entered into with the Flemings, 1 Edw. I., 1272, nearly four centuries before the firm of Messrs. Child & Co. was established as a bank. The second was with Spain and Portugal, 2 Edw. II., 1308. So long a period having elapsed before the great facilities afforded to commerce by banking establishments were suggested to so practical a people as the English, will sufficiently explain the very slow progress made by other nations, which are not celebrated for their practical superiority. The Romans were accustomed to keep banking accounts, and the system of bookkeeping by double entry is said to have been taken from them.* We are surprised that neither the Greeks nor the Romans advanced further than they did—especially the latter, who, we are told, were people of decidedly commercial tendencies. To the Romans must be allowed, without doubt, the invention of transferring a debt by a written document, without the intervention of coined money.

The innumerable changes which have been introduced into the various systems invented for facilitating commercial transactions, adopted by

* Article Argentarii, Smith's 'Dic. Greek and Roman Antiquities.'

different nations during their passage through a
period of seven centuries of time, demonstrate the
enormous difficulties that have to be overcome in
improving and advancing science, which are over-
turned on their march by revolutions, wars, and
innumerable conflicting interests incessantly at
work. The eager interest with which the merchants of all the commercial cities of the world in
these times gather together at fixed days in each
week at their Exchange institutions; the enormous
amount of wealth which is always floating upon
the seas, forming the basis upon which bills of
exchange are drawn, to the extent of hundreds of
millions sterling,* which are circulated into every
corner of the globe, convey an idea of the intricacy
of commerce—not forgetting the different values
and kinds of money which nations have adopted—
and brings forcibly home to us the importance of
well-organised banks.

The first public institution in England par-
taking at all of the nature of a bank was founded
by William I., which he called the Exchequer, from

* It is recorded that in the year 1825, so famous for disastrous
speculations in bubble companies, 400 millions of pounds sterling
were represented by bills of exchange in circulation; such statements, however, are not much to be relied upon.

' scaccum,' a chess-board—a chequered cloth being used with squares upon it resembling those upon a chess-board; so that, when counting the money, the different squares were understood to represent figures corresponding to the amounts placed upon them. With certain modifications, which an existence of 800 years would not fail to produce, it still remains. The Exchequer was originally called ' Scaccarium.' The English and Irish Exchequers were consolidated in 1816.

The various mints which existed prior to the Norman Conquest, and which, in the absence of other places of security, were used as banks of deposit, caused much unnecessary fluctuation in the currency, on account of the removal of these mints from one place to another, according to the caprice of the reigning monarch. Monasteries were considered safe places of deposit, the sacredness of the soil being considered proof against fraud. These mints, with few exceptions, were concentrated by Elizabeth into one, in the Tower of London, which was also used as a depository for cash, in the absence of bankers' strong rooms. This system continued in operation without interruption during the reign of James I.; but Charles I. laid violent hands on the money, and so destroyed

the credit of the Mint in 1640 for ever. The city
merchants and traders were compelled after this
to seek other places of safety, and ultimately
deposited their money with the goldsmiths, who
had settled in Lombard Street, and who possessed
iron safes for their valuables. This was the origin
of banking in England.

Before proceeding to examine the merits of any
particular class of banking institutions such as we
see in the present day, it will perhaps be in better
order to enquire as to the real use of a bank, and
what are the advantages such establishments afford
to the community generally; and whether the
latest period—if we may so term it—of banking-
houses consists of corporations which have been
established with a view honestly to earn their
profits by legitimate banking business.

The use of properly organised and well-managed
banks, and the important position they have held
for so long a period, well justify the remark that
'banking is the hand-maid of commerce;' and it
is by the introduction of such institutions that the
resources of a country are developed and econo-
mised by bringing merchants and traders to settle
their mutual indebtedness without the intervention
of coin.

A bank best serves its own interests, and most rapidly gains a substantial footing with the public, by doing everything—within reasonable bounds—to facilitate commercial operations, and save the time and trouble of those persons who transact their business with it. The use of a bank is principally to take charge of people's money; the first condition being, that the sum deposited for safe custody be returned *when* agreed upon, and secondly, without deduction. We may take it for granted that interest was allowed by banks for money deposited with them in comparatively early times, as we find the word 'interest' in an Act of Parliament passed in the 21st James I., 1623, where it was meant to signify a just compensation for money lent. This Act fixed the rate at 8 per cent. per annum. It was lowered by the Commonwealth to 6 per cent. in 1650, and in 1714, 13th Queen Anne, was reduced to 5 per cent. The restraint of a fixed rate, however, was soon found altogether prejudicial to commerce, and the Acts were repealed by 17 & 18 Vict. c. 90, 1854. Aristotle is said to have stated that as money did not produce money, no equitable claim could be made for interest by the lender. We are told Calvin, the great reformer, was among the first to

show the absurdity of such notions. The founder
of the French Crédit Mobilier, M. Pereire, has
been accused of supporting the theory of a *fixed*
rate of interest. It is high time, however, that
every thinking man discarded such a notion once
for all. Every day that sees mankind become
more enlightened in the science of political
economy, diminishes the number of believers in
the possibility of having a fixed price for that
particular commodity by which the value in
exchange of corn, iron, or coal, is measured.

The use of a bank, then, is not only to take care
of people's money, but to give them something for
the use of it. It would, no doubt, seem natural
when society was not so respectful to the laws of
the country, and people were not characterised by
such a high degree of honesty and integrity, that
capitalists were glad to have their gains safely
taken care of by persons who had iron safes and
strong rooms built for the express purpose, and
perhaps, in some cases, were not unwilling to pay
for the secure custody. Large sums are always
lying at the Bank of England idle even at this
period of our history—*mirabile dictu*—no interest
being allowed by that institution for money that
is placed there upon deposit.

In the most enlightened seats of commerce money fluctuates in price like any other article that is in general use, that is influenced by the laws of supply and demand, and those who have any of it can obtain a price according to the market rate. Banks are the institutions which buy and sell money, and, like corn, or iron, or coal merchants, know the current rate when you apply to them. If you wish to leave money with them, they give you a higher or lower rate of interest per cent. according to circumstances. As a rule, more is allowed for long periods of fixed deposit than short; but some institutions will not allow so much per cent. for a long period as for a short, such rate depending upon the appearance of the market at the moment. There are many different circumstances which influence the price of money, and there are always agencies at work which tend to raise or lower it. The use of banks is to go hand in hand with commerce. They take the money of those who do not know how to employ it, and lend it to those who do, to the advantage of all three classes, and so what before remained idle is now made profitable. Like a thousand little rivulets which run into one mighty stream, and float the commercial navy

of England from London to the sea and distant
climes; so the small depositors make one mighty
sum, that can be employed in agriculture, railways, and a hundred different enterprises by
which all classes are benefited, and the poor man
can approach nearer to the privileges enjoyed
by the rich. The profession of a banker, then,
is to employ the money of other people, as we
have before stated, to the advantage of those more
immediately interested, and for the improvement
of the community generally.

The next great function of a bank, after properly utilising the metallic currency of a country,
is to provide a cheaper and more agreeable form
of currency in the shape of bank-notes. The
great power for good or for evil which is placed
in the hands of banks by allowing them a paper
issue, demonstrates the necessity of some impar-
tial supervision, and we naturally look to the
State—as the highest in authority, and therefore
carrying the greatest weight, both moral and
physical—to control the amount of paper currency which may be put in circulation by banks.
Mr. Ricardo says, p. 214, ' After the establishment
of banks, the State has not the sole power of
coining or issuing money. The currency may as

effectually be increased by paper as by coin; so
that if a State were to debase its money and limit
its quantity, it could not support its value, because
the banks would have an equal power of adding
to the whole quantity of circulation.' Again,
farther on, Mr. Ricardo's opinion of the importance of banks as regards their office as paper-
issuers to the public is conveyed in the following
paragraph: 'A currency is in its most perfect
state when it consists wholly of paper money, but
of paper money of an equal value with the gold
which it professes to represent. The use of paper
instead of gold substitutes the cheapest in place
of the most expensive medium, and enables the
country, without loss to any individual, to exchange all the gold which it before used for this
purpose for raw materials, utensils, and food, by
the use of which both its wealth and its enjoy-
ments are increased.' There are many who object
to the State having anything to do with controlling
the operation of banks or their paper issues; but it
must be borne in mind that there is a wide difference between the State being the issuer and the
State controlling the issues of others. The State
is the highest power that exercises control over
public affairs, and is the motive power—so to

speak—of the empire, acting in obedience to the people's will. It is, therefore, reasonable to suppose that the Government, who are furnished with every assistance in the shape of legal advice, &c., should be the most competent power to control the operations of those institutions which are intrusted to an unlimited extent by the people.

Hear Mr. M'Culloch in his 'Commercial Dictionary,' p. 67, *Necessity of insuring the conversion of bank-notes into coin*: 'The taking of measures to insure the convertibility of bank-notes into coin is a matter which cannot be safely left to the discretion or judgment of individuals, but which must be settled by Government. No bank-notes should be permitted to circulate about the equivalency of which to the coins they profess to represent there can be the smallest room for doubt. It is alleged, indeed, that in this, as in most other things, we may safely trust to the prudence and sagacity of those who deal with banks; and that, if left to themselves, the public will very rarely be deceived. But the widest experience shows that but little if any dependence can be placed on this doctrine. The public is very apt to be misled, in the first instance, in giving confidence to or taking the paper of individuals or associations; and though that were not the case, the condition of an individual or company may change, from bad or expensive management, improvident speculation, unavoidable losses, and fifty other things of which the public know nothing, or nothing certain. The fact that any particular banker who issues paper enjoys the public confidence is at best a presumption merely, and no proof that he really deserves it.' 'There have unfortunately been innumerable instances in which it has turned out that bankers who have long been in the highest credit, and whose notes had been unhesitatingly accepted by the public, have been found to be, on the occurrence of anything to excite suspicion, quite unable to meet their engagements.' From a report on the Extension of the Privilege of the Bank of France, in 1840, we find the following : ' Le droit d'émettre des billets est très avantageux; mais aussi il est si dangereux que l'État doit ou s'en réserver l'exercice ou le régler de manière à en prévenir les abus.' Mr. Ricardo, at p. 408, remarks, ' But if the public require protection against the inferior money which might be imposed upon them by an undue mixture of alloy, and which is obtained by means of the Government stamp when metallic money is used, how much more necessary is such protection when paper money forms the whole, or almost the whole, of the circulating medium of the country? Is it not inconsistent that Government should use its power to protect the community from the loss of one shilling in a guinea, but does not interfere to protect them from the loss of the whole twenty shillings in a one-pound note? In the case of the Bank of England notes, a guarantee is taken by the Government for the notes which the bank issues, and the whole capital of the bank, amounting to more than eleven and a half millions, must be lost before the holders of their notes can be sufferers from any imprudence they may commit, &c. &c.' And again, 'Though I am by no means disposed to judge uncharitably of those who have occasioned so much ruin and distress to the middle and lower classes of the people, yet it must be allowed by the most indulgent, that the true business of banking must be very much abused before it can be necessary for any bank possessing the most moderate funds, to fail in their engagements; and I believe it will be found, in by far the major part of these failures, that the parties can be charged with offences much more grave than those of mere imprudence and want of caution.' M. J. B. Say

also agrees that the interference of Government
is justifiable in two cases; first, to prevent fraud,
and secondly, to certify a fact. ('Économie
Politique,' Book I., chap. xvii.—See also Sir I. B.
Byles on the 'Law of Bills of Exchange, &c.,'
Preface, p. xi.)

The ruin and disaster that can be brought about
by an absence of proper control over banks of
issue—whether exercised by the State or a distinct
corporation—is proved by the crash which took
place among the American banks in 1857, when
all the banks in the Union stopped payment, from
the Gulf of Mexico to the frontiers of Canada.
The kind of security which was demanded of the
American issuing banks may be judged of from
the following extract from a letter of the sub-
secretary of the treasury of the United States,
dated November 27, 1854, which we quote from
Mr. M'Culloch's 'Commercial Dictionary:' ' The
policy of many of the State governments has of
late years consisted in encouraging the issue of
small notes, by sanctioning the establishment of
what are popularly called "free banks," with deposits of stocks and mortgages for the "ultimate"
security of their issues. This "ultimate" security
is, it may be admitted, better than no security at

all. The mischief is, that it *is least available when most wanted*. The very causes which prevent the banks from redeeming their issues promptly cause a fall in the value of the stocks and mortgages, on "the ultimate security" of which their notes have been issued. The "ultimate security" may avail something to the broker who buys them at a discount, and can hold them for months or years; but the labouring man who has notes of these "State security banks" in his possession finds, when they stop payment, that the "ultimate security" for their redemption does not prevent his losing 25 cents, 50 cents, or even 75 cents in the dollar. In a circulating medium we want something more than "ultimate security"—we want also "immediate" security; we want security that is good to-day and will be good to-morrow and the next day, and for ever after. This security is found in gold and silver, and in these only.' If, therefore, banks of issue generally are to be compelled to keep a stock of the precious metals as security against the paper money they issue, there *must* be a controlling power of the very highest order that will keep a constant check upon all banks, and guarantee the community against any loss from the confidence they may place in such institutions.

Good banks add to the wealth of society. A first-class merchant, instead of lending money, gives his name upon paper, which circulates as so much more capital until it is retired. The advantages to be gained by such a process led to the formation of banks of issue, who coined—so to speak—their own credit. The wealth which such banks have amassed is quite inconsiderable as compared with the benefit which has been derived by the community generally, by the addition of so much more capital with which various enterprises have been carried out. The issue of bank-notes forms an entirely distinct increase of capital, beyond that which is furnished by the paper money which is termed bills of exchange and promissory notes; and there is a wide difference between the two classes of paper. The bank-note is circulated entirely upon the faith of the issuing bank, without redress should the bank fail. If it could be proved that a note had been received from A, and that the bank had stopped payment before the recipient B had time to present it, using ordinary diligence, B could legally recover from A; but we believe, in practice, such has seldom succeeded. The bill of exchange is almost always drawn payable at some distant period, and each person hand-

ing a bill of exchange to another has to indorse
it, thereby making himself responsible for the
amount, unless his indorsement be 'without recourse.' Some pass them on immediately; others
retain them for the sake of the interest that
accrues upon them. On the other hand, the note
possesses the advantage of commanding cash at a
moment's notice. The bill, if of first class, may
also do the same, with deduction of interest; but
there is no certainty. Payment by a bill of exchange does not extinguish a debt in the same
way that payment by a bank-note does; until the
bill has arrived at maturity, and has been duly
honoured, all parties to it are liable. Banks being
the great depositories for cash, are naturally always
in possession of large numbers of bills of exchange;
but it does not follow that when they discount these
bills—if they be asked to do so—that they pay, in
cash. English bankers, *as a rule*, only discount
for people who keep their current accounts with
them; and in this manner credit is still further
coined. The amount of the discounted bills, minus
the interest, is placed to the customer's credit, who
draws a cheque for it; this cheque is circulated
as cash through various channels, and returns to
the banker who discounted the bills, never having

been converted into cash at all. Very many banks
have branches in various parts of the country and
abroad, and all banks have agencies at most cities
of importance. By this means payments may be
made simply by the agency of paper all over the
world. A payment of any reasonable sum may
now be made to a bank in London, with orders to
hand it over to a certain firm in Stockholm, and
the whole transaction be completed in three hours.
The use of an English bank, besides affording the
before-mentioned facilities to the public, is to take
care of valuable documents, deeds, and such like;
to collect the money for all documents a customer
may desire to have realised and credited to his
account. The public are disposed also to look upon
their banker as useful in recommending them good
investments. This, however, we are of opinion a
banker should not allow himself to go too far in,
as no banker can keep himself sufficiently 'posted
up' in such matters as to make his advice worth
having; and he may have been ill-informed as to
the nature of this or that security, which will be
sure to cause unpleasantness if his advice be acted
upon.

The four principal sources from which a bank
derives its profit, and in return for which it renders

important services to the public, are the following:
1. The employment of the capital subscribed by
the partners, and upon which the establishment is
based. 2. The current and fixed deposits. 3. The
amount of paper it is able to keep in circulation
in the form of notes. 4. The sum of money which
is constantly *in transitu*, and which, when the business of the bank becomes very large, constitutes
a considerable standing balance. All the money,
therefore, which the bank can obtain by either of
these means, and by all, is employed for discounting, loans, investment in securities which can be
immediately realised in case of urgent pressure for
funds, and cash credits, excepting what must be
kept in the 'till' for immediate use. The amount
required for such purpose can only be judged of
from hour to hour, as the bank works; and this is
one of the most important features in management,
and which requires much experience, depending
upon the nature of the business, and many peculiarities which must be dealt with by the manager
himself.

The real usefulness of a bank has been carried
farther in Scotland than in any other country, so
much encouragement having been given to the
poorer classes to place their small earnings upon

deposit; sums as small as ten pounds having been
for many years received by Scotch banks—a system
which competition at last introduced into England.
The Scotch bankers have from the beginning been
able to afford greater facilities to the lower classes
than the English bankers, as they have derived so
much profit from the issue of their notes, whereas
the London bankers do not enjoy this privilege.

The use of a bank consists in its keeping money
constantly moving, driving it into every possible
channel where it is required, and by this means
stimulating production.

There can be no better instances than those of
banks which have been established in parts of the
country where industry was at a complete stand-
still for want of money, and which have been
worked for some time at a dead loss, until the
stimulus was given time to work its effect, when
the return gradually came, and the bank received
back its own with interest, and subsequently became a flourishing concern. This has taken place
in Scotland, and has been cited in support of an
argument in favour of the issue of small notes,
before a committee of the House of Commons.

The use of a bank is made particularly apparent to persons travelling. Almost any bank will

change the circular notes of another well-known
and respectable bank—without any advice—provided all appears in order.   Large mercantile
houses have, up to the present time, carried on
a system of letters of credit to other merchants in
all parts of the world ; but it is evident that such
business will be better attended to by an institution organised for that purpose, among others ;
and it is quite evident that all such business is by
degrees being absorbed by the banks.   Merchants
are not in the habit of placing a semi-annual or
even annual statement of their position before the
public.   Banks, for their own sakes, are obliged to
do this ; and, although much *may* be concealed
that would injure them, if brought to light, they
can seldom if ever *fail* with such disastrous effect
as a merchant.   The facilities afforded to travel-
lers in the present day by the complete net-work
of banks over almost the whole world, signally
illustrates not only the necessity of advancing
banking as a science, but the importance of its
universal extension as an essential wheel in the
machinery by which the entire commercial system
is kept moving.

    The use of a bank has been increased beyond mea-
sure by the aid of the telegraph.   Bills unprovided

for — through the failure of one or other who should have made provision — may be retired in distant parts of the earth in a few hours, although on the verge of casting a cloud over the maker's credit. Banks in London, with their foreign branches, under a system of telegraphic signals, may be the means of staying a crisis; for many of these popular panics might have been avoided had the foolish terror of people not been aroused by rumours of expected failure, which in many cases have been brought about by the thoughtless rapidity with which people have demanded the return of money lent.

The use of a banker to his client is, that he will always willingly act as a referee, should it be necessary to establish your respectability in the mind of a person to whom you are unknown.

Your banker will collect the money for any and all documents that may come into your hands, and place the proceeds to your account. You draw cheques upon him for any bills you wish to settle, and so he saves you the trouble of counting your money. He pays your subscription to your club, and the premiums for your life and fire policies; undertakes the investment of your surplus funds. If a person wishes to obtain information of an-

other person who keeps a banking account, he
finds immediately that such is impossible from the
banker, unless he keeps an account himself, which
enables him to get the information through his *own*
banker. It is a custom among London bankers,
and no doubt will become universal in course of
time, to give each other such information immediately. Such a system affords to the public an
inestimable advantage, as by such means a dishonest trader soon becomes known, and so got
rid of.

A banker's pass-book affords a complete history
of the expenditure for the year; and those who
have not business habits will find this a great
assistance in controlling their expenditure, at all
events in the aggregate.

By keeping a banker, one has a right to ask of
him or his subordinates a variety of questions with
regard to the best means of remitting money to
distant places, and other matters, which otherwise
might cause much trouble in obtaining.

The use of a bank assists most materially in
dispelling the notion that wealth consists in money.
This idea has existed for an incredible period in
the minds of men, who by a little reflection could
have so easily got rid of it. Adam Smith destroyed

it in the minds of all men who were willing to
study his arguments; and now the question no
longer even causes a dispute. The gold which
lies still in the bank is of no more use than the ore
from which it is coined; it only becomes wealth
when it is circulated, and by such circulation
assists production. Much gold lies *always* still in
the vaults of the Bank of England. It may be
thought that this fact upsets our argument; but
if a certain amount of specie forms the pivot
around which twice as much in paper circulates,
it is more productive by the proportion, than if it
were in active circulation itself—leaving out of the
calculation the loss caused by using so costly a
material. Gold is the chosen representative of
wealth; that commodity by which the value in
exchange of everything else is measured, by reason
of its being more suitable than any other substance, for more reasons than because it varies so
little in cost of production, and, consequently, in
value in exchange, and also presents the greatest
worth in a more convenient form than any other
product of the earth. This representative of
wealth it is the object of banks to keep constantly
moving, which is more and more productive just
in proportion as it is kept in circulation without

ceasing. As the maxim among shopkeepers is, small profits and quick returns, so for a bank to combine profit with safety, it should keep whatever funds it may have for employment always on the move; never out beyond reach for too long periods at a time.

Doctor Adam Smith says, that the advantages to be derived from the establishment of banks may be compared to the profit which would be obtained from converting our highways into corn fields, and procuring a road through the air.

The most important addition to the facilities which banking institutions have invented for themselves, to enable them to adjust their mutual indebtedness without the trouble of presenting separately for payment the cheques or bills which one bank may hold payable at another bank, was the Clearing-house, which was established by the principal bankers in London in the year 1775. The system pursued is so simple that, suffice it to say, when the clerks of two different banks wish to exchange the cheques one may have upon the other, the balance—in whosesoever favour it may be—is paid by a cheque on the Bank of England, where every banker has an account. In the beginning the banks with the aid of the Clearing-

house were enabled to adjust several millions
sterling of mutual indebtedness, employing only a
few hundred thousand pounds; the mode of settlement, however, has now become so simplified that
neither notes nor coin is required at all. It is
only quite lately that the Bank of England entered
the Clearing-house.

CHAPTER II.

TWO CLASSES OF BANKS.

BANKS may be divided into two classes—private banks, and joint-stock banks with, and without, limited liability. Formerly private banks could not have more than six partners. By the Act of Parliament 39 & 40 Geo. III. c. 28, section 15, no bank was allowed to be established whose partners should exceed six in number, ' to borrow, owe, or take up any sum or sums of money, on their bills or notes, payable on demand, or at any less time than six months from the borrowing thereof.' Later on, in the year 1826, an Act of Parliament, of 7 Geo. IV. c. 46, was passed, which allowed banking corporations to be established consisting of more than six persons; but they were not allowed to transact their business within sixty-five miles of London, and were prohibited from having any branch establishment in the city of London. Every member of a banking corporation

established under this Act was responsible for
every and all its acts and deeds.

There are many provisions still unrepealed
which affect banking corporations which have not
been registered under the Joint-Stock Companies
Acts of 1857 or 1862, or have not been incorporated by letters patent under the 7 & 8 Vict.
c. 113. This last Act was passed in the year 1844,
and gave permission to banks whose corporations
consisted of more than six persons, and which had
been established before May 6, to apply for letters
patent, by which they could be incorporated under
this Act. The 7 & 8 Vict. c. 113, gave to banking
companies established within sixty-five miles of
London, and incorporated on and after May 6,
1844, the great privilege of suing and being sued
in the names of their public officers, provided they
complied with the Act in other respects, by making the returns required. In 1857, however, the
Act was repealed, and not till 1862 were the provisions for the banks suing and being sued in the
names of their public officers re-enacted.

The latest Act of Parliament, that of 1862,
affecting the establishment of banks, makes the
following prohibitions in section 4:

1. No partnership of more than ten persons is

to be formed for banking purposes, unless it is
registered under the Act, or is formed under some
other Act of Parliament or letters patent; and,

2. No partnership of more than twenty persons
is to be formed for the acquisition of gain, unless
it is registered under the Act, or is formed under
an Act of Parliament or letters patent, or unless
it is formed for working mines within the juris-
diction of the stannaries; in fact, a cost-book
mining company.

Banking corporations established under the
7 & 8 Vict. c. 113, who neglected to register
before January 1, 1858, might be sued, but
were unable to sue either in equity or at law.
Managers and directors were subject to a penalty
of 5l. for every day that elapsed after the registration should have been made, and the shareholders
could receive no dividend. The above omissions,
however, did not make the bank illegal.

Banking corporations registered under 20 &
21 Vict. c. 49, were required to register under
the Companies Act of 1862, except the liability of
their shareholders was limited by letters patent or
Act of Parliament. Not having complied with the
demands of the Act 20 & 21 Vict. c. 49, laid them
open to the penalties above-named also.

In the year 1858 an Act was passed, 21 & 22
Vict. c. 91, which permitted banking corporations
to be established with limited liability, under the
Joint-Stock Companies Act of 1857. All other
banks could make the liability of their shareholders
limited, excepting in regard to their issue of notes;
and for this they must remain unlimited, by registering under the Act. It was necessary, however,
to make due publication of the fact, that all who
kept accounts or had other business with the bank
might be made acquainted with the change, and
withdraw if they chose. The bank was also obliged
to publish periodically a statement of its assets
and liabilities.

Many banking companies, consisting of seven
members or more, as is well known, have singly
and with others become limited companies under
the above Act. They are compelled, however,
before registration, to obtain the consent of the
majority of their members at a general meeting—
the only alteration required in the name of a
company registering under the Limited Liability
Act being the addition of the word 'limited.'

Private banks, of six or ten members, may still
carry on their business without being required to
register themselves as banking companies; but,

without registration, the liability of the members cannot be 'limited.'

On its being proposed to start a banking company on the 'limited liability' principle, it is required that at least seven persons must sign a deed of association, having the following particulars contained therein: 1. The objects of the company; 2. The company's name, attaching the word 'limited' at the end; 3. A statement that the members' liability is limited; 4. Naming the place where the office of the company is to be situated; 5. The amount of each share, and total amount of the capital, with other particulars specified in the Act in detail.

A manager or director, who endorses or accepts a bill for a bank registered under the Limited Liability Act, without including the word 'limited,' becomes personally liable thereon.

From 1708 to 1826, the Bank of England was the only bank in London that could be established with more than six partners.

Private banks have formerly been worked upon the basis of a capital subscribed by not more than six persons, which, if one of whom die, his proportion has been withdrawn, unless any member of his family should succeed to his interest in the

concern. As a rule, all the partners in a private
bank contribute to its administration; and it has
long been a matter of dispute as to whether private
banks under this system have not been more suc-
cessful, in proportion to their means, than a joint-
stock bank under the administration of salaried
servants. It appears on the face of it reasonable
that any business will be more lucrative when
those who are directly interested in every one per
cent. of extra profit are constantly on the look-out
to take advantage of any lucrative investment that
may present itself, or to secure the business of this
or that firm or company. Mr. J. Stuart Mill, in
his 'Principles of Political Economy,' bk. ii.,
p. 486, says: 'Management, however, by hired
servants, who have no interest in the result but
that of preserving their salaries, is proverbially
inefficient, unless they act under the inspecting
eye, if not the controlling hand, of the person
chiefly interested; and prudence almost always
recommends giving to a manager not thus controlled a remuneration partly dependent on the
profits, which virtually reduces the case to that of
a sleeping partner.' It will be seen, however, that
a manager whose remuneration depends upon the
profit will be very likely to engage in transactions

of a less secure nature than the partner of a private
bank, whose fortune is at stake. A manager's
income may also be at stake; but it is a natural
and reasonable conclusion, that there can be no
such controlling power constantly keeping his
operations in check, as when his income and capital
also are endangered by engaging in hazardous
business.

Private banks may be looked upon now as
institutions of the past. A couple of years even
has seen many of the best of them swallowed
up by the joint-stock system; and there can be
no doubt which is the better suited to our
times.

A joint-stock bank differs from a private bank—
First, by its capital being permanent; secondly, its
number of partners unlimited; and thirdly, in the
form of its government. If a partner—or, as he
is generally termed, a shareholder—die, his shares
are simply transferred, and the capital undergoes
no alteration. A joint-stock bank is directed by a
board of gentlemen, drawn from various classes of
society, under whom is a manager, who acts as
their representative to the public, and who, under
their control, administers the whole of the affairs
of the bank, assisted by a sub-manager, secretary,

and subordinates, as the nature of the business may require.

Up to the year 1855,* shareholders in joint-stock banks were unlimited in their liability, by which system it will be seen that many rich men would be liable for their entire fortunes by becoming shareholders; and thus, banks of unlimited liability, on coming into positions of difficulty, would be likely to lose their best shareholders, as was often the case in the outset, when masters transferred their shares into the names of their servants. This, however, was put an end to by a special clause, which all banking copartnerships take care to include in their regulations, and which empowers the directors of a bank to refuse a transfer should they not approve of the transferee.

The Act of Parliament passed in 1855, limiting the liability of shareholders—not banks—to the amount of their shares, is looked upon by many us in principle vicious. There can be no doubt that a great number of banks, established with limited liability, have failed most disastrously both in England and America. The latter country especially has caused more ruin than any other

* Limited Liability Act, 20 & 21 Vict. c. 49.

by the stoppage of her banks, which are nearly, if not all, on the limited liability system. Some assert, with reason, that limiting the shareholders' liability takes off much of the pressure which should be constantly kept upon those whose duty it is to exercise caution and prudence in employing the bank's funds. Shareholders whose *all* is at stake, will see that prudent and experienced directors form the board, and a strict supervision will be insured, down to the clerks in the office.

There is great danger of a new bank getting itself and all connected with it into inextricable trouble when it does not at an early stage realise the hopes of its projectors; and how very often has this been the case! How many lamentable windings-up have we seen; how much endless disputing have we seen at general meetings, ending in friends becoming enemies; how many complicated law cases have filled the newspapers, placing in prominent relief misguided and inexperienced directors; how many unfortunate officers of all grades have been allured into the vortex by a few extra hundreds a year! Each new bank that comes out is always going to be such a grand success. All sorts of business will flow in as soon as the offices are opened. The prospects are so

bright, the preliminary expenses are begun with a
light heart, and all goes well for a year or so, until
the actors in so many of these unfortunate cases
realise the delusion into which they have been led.

There is a great deal of romance that hangs
round the starting of a new bank. There is too
much distance between the present hopefulness
and the future stern difficulties. There is no
more royal road to banking profits than to any
other sort of profits; and it is one of the most
singular peculiarities in connection with men who
have had much experience in other walks of trade,
as merchants, &c., that they are as easily deluded
into believing that a bank *must* be a success when
it is brought out with a certain *éclat*, and the
shares are well taken up, as younger men with
much less experience. There is so much dust
thrown into men's eyes by the opinions of others
who, in the goodness of their hearts, wish to see
all mankind pleased with any projects they may
have in hand. In all these enterprises there is a
great deal too much taken for granted, and trusted
to chance, where matters should be properly investigated. In establishing a bank there is such
a multitude of people interested, and so much
property that must be lost in case of failure, that

such projects should not be left too much uncontrolled in the hands of a few, whose self-inte-
restedness is so likely to lead them to disregard
the real interests of others. There is a good deal
of what is termed 'kudos' attaching to the office
of director; and there are very few persons, unless their thirst for notoriety has been somewhat
satiated, who have sufficient self-denial to refuse
to become directors, when they inwardly know
they bring *only* what prestige their name may
have gained in any other walk in life to support
the bank. Some men who have had nothing to
do with banks before certainly *may* make good
directors, but the danger always is that directors
who are comparative novices will want to meddle
too much in the management—possibly with the
best of motives; but when certain functions are
expected of certain people, and others who have
a right to interfere by virtue of the position
of director assume even occasionally those functions, then they do not weigh with due responsibility upon any one, and what should be some
one's business becomes no one's. There can be
nothing so injurious to the proper management
of a bank as *certain* responsibilities not being
fixed upon *certain* people. What is every one's

E

business is no one's; and where money of all
things is dealt in, and its loss made possible by
an absence of proper organisation, no establishment, having such inherent defects, can expect to
obtain any position in the public estimation, or
to succeed. Every officer should have a defined
position written and agreed upon, and when each
part is perfect the whole will be.

PERNICIOUS EFFECTS OF TOO MUCH COMPETITION IN COMMERCE AND BANKING—PROPOSED CHECK.

The facilities which in these times are afforded
by the numerous banks and companies to any one
with the smallest means who chooses to dabble in
business matters, foster to a most hurtful extent
those elements which have for some time past
acted most injuriously against the steady and
natural fluctuation in the price of credit and
capital in this country. The broad area of commercial affairs has of late years been immeasurably
extended, with undue and unsafe rapidity. The
new ground has been occupied by saplings, which
in many, if not most cases, strike out into extensive engagements before their roots have got hold
of the ground, and are swept away by the first
breath which may be produced by unexpected

agitation in the commercial world. New companies, which are supported by the profits derived
from such sources, may survive a few summers;
but when the traders, upon whose business their
existence depends, are struggling to establish
themselves upon ground that is already occupied,
they can only expect a brief career, progressing
to a certain point which will not be considered
satisfactory by the shareholders for any length of
time, and the inevitable winding up will be the
only course left open.

To decide to what extent precisely, both banks
and merchants can be established with benefit
to themselves and the community at large, is a
matter which is beyond the capacity of almost
any tribunal; but it appears strange that commercial disorders follow one upon the other, without doubt most materially influenced by the evil to
which I allude, without arousing the serious attention of those who are so damaged and occasionally
ruined by its effects.

There are so many ways in which the eyes of
the public may be blinded to the real position
which a firm occupies, that it seems almost in-
comprehensible that merchants generally — most
of whom we may presume wish to see their

profession exalted, and the mercantile community
in their own country signalised by a system which
will exclude incompetent and we may say dishonest persons from interfering with the proper
and legitimate fluctuations in the rate of interest
charged for the use of capital, &c.—do not combine for the purpose of checking and endeavour-
ing to remove so great an obstacle to the progress
of sound commercial business.

Now that the merchants and trading ranks of
all denominations are so much increased, it stands
to reason that a larger number of eyes and hands
are incessantly watching and ready to grasp any
description of business by which a profit may be
made; and in consequence the profit upon almost
everything is lowered by incessant competition,
and the means by whose aid all business is
carried on are raised to a higher price by the
increased number who seek its assistance.

Political economy tells us, that populations increase in proportion to the means of subsistence.
Pestilences and plagues occasionally sweep numbers from the face of the earth, and we may rea-
sonably conclude that such means are employed
by the Almighty for regulating the increase of
mankind when they progress beyond the capacity

of the land where they are born to support them.
A commercial crisis sweeps away the weak merchants who will make business in places beyond
the capacity of those places to support them.
The discretion of man in both cases being too
little exercised, he loses sight of those principles
by which his actions should be governed.

The undue increase in the number of merchants
and traders must of necessity exercise a hurtful
influence, sooner or later, upon those institutions
whose business it is to furnish credit and capital
to those who may require it. An increased number of applicants raises the price, and more lending institutions are established, which in their
turn encourage speculative and dangerous trading,
and in this way every department of the commercial system becomes weakened by too rapid and
not sufficiently consolidated extension; and when
any at all exceptional causes are at work to
agitate mercantile affairs, the weak houses not
only ruin themselves but bring down the institutions who encouraged their efforts, and whose
existence in a measure depended upon their
support.

The last few years have shown the high rate to
which 'interest' has been forced in the London

market, by more than one cause, not the least of
which is the great competition for accommodation which is constantly pressing upon the market.
We have seen on several occasions, when the minimum interest charged by the Bank of England
has receded to a moderate rate, a legion of under-
takings, which have been waiting their opportunity, press forward ; and the only means of driving
them off is by making the charge more than they
can bear. In extreme cases of disorder, of whatever nature, the first suggestion that presses itself
upon us is, to contrive a combination of forces
that will overcome and destroy whatever evil
effects we may desire to get rid of. Banks as a
body are established not only for the benefit and
profit of those who establish them, but for the
general convenience and assistance of all classes
of the community. In quiet times when all works
well and smoothly, the banks are left to make the
most of their opportunities ; but it is also expected
by the public that they should at the same time
not forget that the period will arrive when they
must be prepared to assist and protect their sup-
porters. This is only reasonable ; and passing over
any comments as to how far certain institutions
have fallen short of what was expected of them in

this respect, we come to the question of how far is it possible for the future to provide against similar shortcomings. There can be little doubt that in banking, as in most other professions whose institutions are governed by certain fixed principles, which they are more or less all bound to follow, the safest system upon which they can proceed is that of *co-operation*.

It is related, and we believe truly, that certain Scotch banks are now in existence from their having adopted a system of co-operation at the first appearance of a 'run.' As an instance: a suspicion has been known to have arisen against a certain bank in Scotland, which caused a rapid 'run' on its deposits. Immediately the depositors obtained their money, and were outside the bank, they knew not what to do with it, and were found as a rule to place it in the nearest bank they came to. The bank receiving the funds of these panic-stricken depositors knew full well that unless the 'run' upon the first bank were immediately arrested, their own deposits would inevitably follow; the consequence was, that the funds brought by the frightened depositors were instantly returned to the besieged bank by one of the receiving bank's clerks. By such an

arrangement it will be evident that a ' run ' may
be most easily disposed of—instead of allowing
a probably groundless feeling of distrust, which
may take its rise from the most trifling and
absurd causes, to grow to such dangerous dimensions ; and it is not unlikely that numbers of the
depositors, had they known the real origin of the
alarm, would, instead of following the stream, have
assisted the banks with further sums, rather than
have withdrawn what they had already deposited.
The age we live in, and the experience we have
already had of banking, must have convinced
most persons that no bank can, or is expected to
be organised and worked to be at all times prepared to meet such sudden and crushing demands
as these catastrophes produce, and that when
merchants and capitalists of means know the
position of the respective banks with whom they
do business, to be sound, and from whom they
obtain great facilities in ordinary times, they
should rise above the level of forsaking them
when times of pressure and distrust—which must
occasionally happen to every concern—are weighing
upon them.

Most shareholders in banks also keep their
accounts with the banks in whose dividend they

are interested; and as they are, as a matter of
course, anxious that the dividend should be as
large as it can be consistently with safety, they
wish to see the banks cleverly managed—managed so that all the spare funds are kept constantly employed, and that by their judicious
and cautious arrangements as much as possible of
other people's money should be intrusted to them
for employment. In order, however, that all the
funds which are constantly flowing into the bank
from many sources should be employed, investments for comparatively long periods—such as six
months—must be made, or the banks would be
unable in ordinary times to 'place' their money,
and prevent a loss of interest. It will be seen,
then, that a bank upon a large scale which is
compelled to receive vast sums—a good proportion of which it engages to return on demand
—has not a fair chance allowed it when its
shareholders, who take in quiet times the benefit derived from placing a certain proportion of
such demand liabilities at longer periods in
order to obtain a higher rate of interest, when
the abnormal pressure comes, expect the bank
to help itself how it can; to collect at once these
six-month loans, and meet all the obligations,

which by its pretensions it certainly engages
to do.

Mr. James Wilson made the following remarks
upon this question in the 'Economist' paper, in
the year 1845, which are quite worthy of reference. We are not able to give the number of the
paper in which they appeared, but that is of no
particular moment.

'The two great essential and fundamental principles, therefore, on which the success of banking
depends, and to which hitherto very little attention has been paid in all the discussions which
have taken place on the subject, are :

'1st. By what means can a bank attract the
largest amount of deposits?

'2nd. In what way can a bank employ those
deposits to the greatest advantage, consistently
with the conditions on which they are made; that
is, repayment on demand?

'These two propositions really do involve the
whole art of banking, whether viewed as a source
of profit to bankers, or as a source of economy,
safety, and convenience to the public. We will
consider them separately.

'First. By what means can a bank attract the
largest amount of deposits?

'The first essential property which a bank must possess is a perfect confidence on the part of the public. The small amount of benefit which a banker can afford to give his customer for placing his money in his hands can never be sufficient to induce any man to run a hazard; and, more particularly, the mere difference of terms which one banker can afford compared with another cannot be sufficient to induce any man to give preference to more tempting terms, when weighed against a greater security and confidence.

'The want of this confidence, to a sufficient extent, and for a sufficiently long and uninterrupted period, has done more to injure the business of banking in England than any other circumstance. In this respect, and in the effect which the absence of confidence has exerted over the amount and character of the deposits of English banks, we discover a striking contrast between them and the banks of Scotland. Much of this fundamental defect in the character of English banks, if not all, we believe can be traced to the effects of legislation. Since the Bank of England was erected into a corporation, the restrictions which the Government has from time to time imposed on the exercise of capital and the independent efforts of

individuals, whether singly or in a combined
form, in order to preserve the privileges of that
establishment, we believe to have been the root
of much if not all of the mischief and discredit
which has attached to the banking practice of
England. But for the peculiar privileges granted
to the Bank from time to time, but for the restrictions thus placed on private enterprise, and
the constant interference of the Government to
tinker and patch up evils to which their own
previous acts had led, there can be no doubt
whatever that many years ago we should have
had our banking establishments placed on the
highest, safest, and most beneficial principles
which free competition, intellect, and energy
could suggest and carry into practice. Banking,
above all other professions, is that which under
entire freedom and non-interference would soonest
be placed in the most perfect position. The
public will not employ an unsafe bank while they
have those of perfect safety with which they can
deal, and who are ready to afford them all the
facilities which banks can do. It may be said
that some men, who are chiefly borrowers, have
no choice with which bank they can deal. But to
suppose that bad banks could be supported by

borrowers, with an indifferent credit, is absurd.
It is the *lenders* and not the *borrowers*, and least
of all the *inferior borrowers*, that constitute the
strength and power of banks. We know what
has been the result of the restrictions imposed on
banking by the law in this country, and we have
only to look to Scotland to see what has been the
effect of a long career of perfect freedom and competition upon the character and credit of the
banking establishments of that country, as well
as in affording the greatest convenience and satis-
faction to the public.'

The second proposition which Mr. Wilson sub-
mits for solution carries the assumption that all
deposits are '*repayable on demand.*' Now, no bank
accepts more than it can help, repayable on demand; or, I may say, a bank always prefers
deposits with some days' notice of withdrawal.
Neither do the depositors, in many cases, wish to
place their money on these conditions, as they are
not and cannot be allowed so much interest—as
a rule—as when they give the banker a certain
period of notice of withdrawal. A large proportion of every bank's deposits must necessarily be
payable on demand, if they wish to have the accounts of merchants and such like, who can only

deal with them upon such conditions; as the
nature of a merchant's business necessitates his
having a certain sum of money at his immediate
disposal. This convenience can be granted to the
merchant, and at the same time a certain return,
in the shape of interest, for the use of his credit
balance; and such a system works exceedingly
well in quiet times, as what one client draws
another pays in, and so the two streams, with
varying but generally moderate fluctuations, according to the activity which may exist and the
employment that can be found for capital, neu-
tralise each other, so far as to leave a proportion of
from two-thirds to three-fourths, which the banker
may safely employ without unjustifiable risk. This
proportion, of course, varies in favour of the
bank, as its transactions increase.

While every other bank looks upon the Bank of
England as the responsible institution, as holding
the metallic basis upon which the credit of the
country is maintained, it cannot be expected that
the directors of other banks will interest themselves in providing a system of co-operation to the
same extent as they would were a general council
organised, to which every bank and financial institution of importance was compelled to send a

member. Banking has so enormously expanded
of late years that it will be found ere long that a
complete reformation must be brought about, if
the serious disturbances which commercial affairs
occasionally drift into are to be handled and dealt
with in such a manner that we are not held up
to be ridiculed by the world. If a council were
formed, at which each board of directors—having
a certain status—was compelled to have one member present, and all boards would naturally choose
the most enlightened and forward member of their
body; at the approach of disturbances an immense
and incalculable power to avert the mischievous
results of over-trading and dishonest speculation
would be at the disposal of the mercantile community and of the banking profession. By the
establishment of such a council, the antagonistic
feelings, which we have too great reason to believe
exert at the present time a very hurtful influence
over the progress of banking, might be to a great extent assuaged. In order to effect such an object, so
that it might work harmoniously in itself, and the
members of such council be in a position calmly
and with matured judgment to deliberate upon
the course to be pursued under any circumstances,
every feeling of jealousy would have to be set aside.

There are a few large banks at the present time in London which have so consolidated their position that they may possibly be strong enough to stand alone under almost any pressure that can arise. Such institutions might refuse to attend such a council, for the reason stated; but if the presence of members from these large and influential establishments would give—which there can be no doubt they would—an elevating tone to the tribunal, which would require all the prestige and importance that could be collected, in order that its edicts might carry sufficient weight to influence the whole profession in following their advice, proposals for their co-operation should be so made as to insure their acceptance. The only council which has a recognised superiority, and which has taken upon itself to announce the rate of interest which the borrowing British public must pay from time to time, is the court of directors of the Bank of England. This corporation has, through a long series of years, gradually acquired a predominating power from its connection with the State; but the State merely employs this establishment as its banker, without exercising any influence whatever over the choice of its directors. It may easily be conceived, that in this

manner there can be no guarantee that the best
men are ever allowed a voice in the consideration
of the rate of interest. The public journals, however, especially the 'Economist,' 'Times,' and
'Daily News,' keep so close upon the heels of the
bank court, that a false step on their part is immediately published by the press; and we may con-
gratulate ourselves that so powerful a check upon
their proceedings is already in existence.

The great advantage of the council I propose
would be, that in times of extreme pressure, when
an immense proportion of the country's capital
was locked up; when vast sums lay invested in
raw materials, which would probably experience
much difficulty in realisation immediately there
was any prospect of severe tightness in the market,
a wide and extensive general knowledge of the
position and standing of all houses at that particular period would be necessary, in order to avoid
refusal of assistance to perfectly sound although
temporarily embarrassed houses; for, notwithstanding the dishonest speculation which thoroughly
bad and capitalless houses have practised from
time to time, to the injury of those who were probably quite justified in anticipating that they would
have been able to realise the commodities in which

F

their funds were at that period locked up, such
fluctuations *may* arise in the earth's produce, and
such contingencies may happen that, as far as we
know or are able to calculate at present, no human
foresight can render perfect the provision against
such irregularities ; and, consequently, the want
in such times is a power composed of the most
efficient and experienced persons, to judge whether
those who seek assistance have really come into
their difficulties by reason of natural causes, which
human foresight cannot provide against; as it is
beyond dispute that mercantile houses, by favour-
itism and manœuvring, obtain at times immense
assistance to enable them to cover losses which
have been occasioned by the most unjustifiable
speculation, by engaging in a class of business
which, under no circumstances, or at any time,
they had a right to meddle with ; and by this
means they obtain relief which cannot be given to
two at the same time, and is therefore certainly
employed, in one case, in encouraging a class of
speculation which, when carried on by numbers, so
materially stimulates the evil which can be miti-
gated, in a measure, when due only to normal
causes, and is most probably (at all events possibly)
denied to a more modest and upright firm, whose

operations are affected by what they may be powerless to control.

The tribunal who should deliberate upon the course to be adopted when the mercantile horizon predicts serious changes for the worse—for these great commercial disorders never happen without those previous signs which are so surely premonitory of mischief—should be composed of men whose cautious judgment has led them successfully through the shoals and quicksands which commerce presents at all points. These men are comparatively rare, and, consequently, whether in large commercial houses or banking and financial institutions, soon work their way to the surface by the exhibition of those qualities which constitute their superiority, and which would render their selection a matter of no difficulty. By the formation of this body or tribunal, which should be composed of men who have had experience in not only banking, but all the great branches of commerce, many complicated questions, which are now tediously discussed through the leading journals, might be debated and elucidated for the public benefit.

I would propose that this tribunal be composed of at least one hundred members, each of whom would be subject to re-election every year; and that

every person engaged in banking, financial, and
mercantile affairs—having attained his majority—
should be entitled to one vote, irrespective of his
position, means, connection, or attainments; and
that his vote be not transferable. The benefit to the
community generally would depend upon this tribunal being composed of members of every branch;
by that, I mean men who have had wide experience
in the fluctuations of every article of produce imported or exported, and also a knowledge of the
chief importers and exporters, so that the banks,
as a body, might, through the medium of this tribunal, receive a warning of any important change
that was expected which might seriously embarrass certain houses. Those, for instance, whose
suspension had become inevitable, in consequence
of an immense and unforeseen fall in certain produce which they held, would have a claim to assistance—against approved security—by a proper
representation of their position, provided always
such applicants were previously known to be people
of good reputation, and whose statements would
warrant a further enquiry. In this manner much
good might be effected, such precautions being
taken before matters had proceeded too far.
Timely assistance not only prevents the fall of

one house, but generally the almost certain fall
of others engaged with it ; and, what is still worse,
prevents an unjust suspicion being cast upon those
whose position may be perfectly sound, and de-
prives them of the accommodation usually afforded ;
and thus the disturbance grows, and assumes by
degrees proportions, whose calamitous results we
are already too much acquainted with.

This tribunal should have a large hall erected
in the city of London—the capital of the country
— where the members who were chosen could
devote with ease and comfort the time required of
them. An alphabetical register should be kept by
officers, in which should be recorded the particulars
of every firm in the city—how much capital they
took into the business, and what business they
were engaged in.

Such conditions as these could be lengthened,
of course, with advantage ; and, in justice to the
trading community, some book of public reference
should exist to prevent the present vague and
uncertain information which is alone obtainable
upon such matters.

There are many firms which look upon themselves as private altogether, and who do a business
as large and larger than some banks. Their

liabilities are also frequently greater to the public,
and their failure would be more disastrous than
that of any bank, and yet they never publish a
balance-sheet. They may go on doing a large
trade for years, all the time in the most unsound
condition, striving in the most unpardonable manner by new speculations to retrieve lost ground;
and it is by this sort of thing that the calamitous
effects of a crisis are made much more than they
need be. If a tribunal, such as the one I speak of,
were accessible to any member of the community,
through which he could demand enquiry if he had
sufficient reason to know that matters had proceeded too far, and by which he could compel any
firm to produce a statement of their position
without giving up his name, a service would be
rendered to trade and mercantile affairs generally,
the beneficial effects of which are beyond calculation. Should such a circumstance arise as that a
firm had been unjustly suspected, it would remain
in the power of the tribunal not only to sponge
from their name the least suspicion which the
enquiry might have occasioned, but to inform the
public that Messrs. So & So were in every respect
sound, and that their transactions were proved to
have been characterised by the most unsullied

integrity. Banks and many other institutions have periodically to show their position to the public, even when organised in all respects in the most complete way yet invented, and whose operations are conducted upon those principles which do not include any speculative elements. How much more necessary must it be to establish some system for keeping a watchful check upon merchant houses which show no balance-sheet, and whose operations, in the majority of cases, are much more intricate than those of a bank, and are directed by a judgment which seldom errs on the side of prudence.

There will—I doubt not—be many who will pronounce this scheme at once impracticable, on the ground alone that the community would never submit their affairs to be investigated at the dictation of any one or more individuals, who might possibly be actuated by base motives; but I maintain, nevertheless, that the establishment of such an institution—defective as it might be at the outset—would be found, by its power to control or exclude injurious and reckless operators, of incalculable service in purifying the stream of British commerce, and would tend, in course of time, to improve the *morale* of the entire mercantile community.

CHAPTER III.

OF BANKING ACCOUNTS.

As to choosing a Banker—Of opening an Account - Of the differ<n:t
sorts of Accounts—General Observations.

BEFORE deciding on the commencement of business
with any particular banker, a prudent man will
necessarily be anxious to know something of the
stability of the establishment to which he is about
to commit such important trusts.

In the metropolis, where banks are so numerous
and of such very high standing, a mistake can
hardly be made; but in the provinces the difficulty
is greater, as, excepting the larger towns, the
choice is generally restricted to three or four
establishments; sometimes less.

The periodical publication of accounts by the
joint-stock banks furnishes a very important element in coming to a decision, although, in several
notorious instances, the figures given have been
utterly fallacious; still we are proud to believe

that these are exceptional cases, and that a published balance-sheet is a reliable document.

In agricultural districts the private banker is usually a landed proprietor; and from this a fair idea of his individual wealth may be formed. In manufacturing towns a trade is frequently combined with the business of a banker; and the question may fairly arise as to what portion of the resources of the bank are withdrawn to meet the requirements of the trade. It appears to us that the private banker labours under a disadvantage in competition with his joint-stock opponent—in this way, that the publication at stated times of the accounts of the latter gives confidence to the public, whilst the transactions of the former are shrouded in mystery.

With the joint-stock bank, in case of misfortune, there is the balance of capital that has not been called up to fall back upon; but the whole of the private banker's capital will doubtless have been lost ere he will decide upon closing his doors.

Again, although at some time or other a private bank may have been in possession of ample means, still, by the retirement of partners, and consequent withdrawal of their capital, its resources may be weakened to a great extent—a fact of which the great body of customers would be ignorant; and, of course, it would be to the interest of the bank that they should not be informed.

So, again, on the death of a banker having a family, he bequeaths the business to one of his sons, and very probably the bulk of his property is withdrawn, to be divided amongst his other children—he to whom the bank descends simply getting the hive from which others have extracted the honey.

We should always distrust establishments offering high rates of interest. Such a method of doing business is only to be made profitable by travelling out of the usual safe paths; the customer who has the temerity to accept such inducements is but too likely to lose his interest and endanger his principal.

Bankers, before opening an account with a new customer, usually require an introduction, if the individual be a stranger.

The person who introduces a customer to a bank is expected to have some knowledge both of the state of his friend's monetary affairs and of his moral respectability.

One reason for this caution is very obvious, viz. the banker's own protection.

Another, which does not appear so plainly to the casual observer, is this; that the fact of a man having an account with a first-rate banker, is to a certain extent accepted as a guarantee, that, in the opinion of the banker, his customer is a person worthy of some trust; and such being the case, if bankers accept indiscriminately, and without enquiry, all accounts offered to them, the public will give them credit for precautions which they do not adopt, and will in consequence be deceived.

Bankers usually object to open accounts with executors or trustees (as such). The difficulty is, however, easily got over, by taking the names of the parties individually.

It is necessary, before opening an account in the name of a married woman, to have the written authority of the husband for so doing.

It is not considered a good thing, except under extraordinary circumstances, for commercial houses to change their bankers; nor do bankers look very favourably on customers who do business with more than one house. In the case of a very large business, it is sometimes done from prudential motives.

There are three classes of accounts with which banks have to deal, viz. :—

Credit Accounts,
Overdrawn Accounts, and
Deposit Accounts.

Of these, the first-named is by far the largest,
and, in fact, the only one of which the Bank of
England, and most, if not all, the London private
bankers take cognisance.

It is simply an account in which the customer
always has a balance standing to his credit.

Overdrawn accounts, or, as they are sometimes
called, 'cash credits,' are not unusual with country
bankers. They are worked in the same way as
credit accounts; but the balance is always or
generally in favour of the banker, who takes
security from his customer, and gives him a 'limit,'
beyond which he must not draw. The difference
between this method and an ordinary advance, as
made by London bankers, is, that in the latter
case a certain sum is placed for a stated time to
the customer's credit, and either repaid at the
expiration of that time or renewed for a further
period; but with overdrawn accounts, only the
sum required is drawn, and on that alone interest
is charged. Such arrangements may continue for
years without the balance ever being a credit-
balance.

Deposit accounts, from which banks derive a large portion of the funds wherewith they carry on their business, are sums placed at stated rates of interest with a bank, for which receipts are given, called deposit receipts. These are not transferable, and must be produced and signed on the back previous to the repayment of the money. The usual rate of interest allowed on these deposits by the joint-stock banks of London is 1 per cent. under the minimum rate of discount at the Bank of England for the time being, the banks making their profit by the margin. When any alteration is made in the rate allowed, it is usual to give notice by advertisements in the 'Times,' and other daily papers. As we before observed, the Bank of England and the London private banks eschew this business. In the country, however, the private banks (especially in the manufacturing districts, where money can generally be profitably employed in discounting) encourage it. It is not difficult to see how, in the cases of overdrawn and deposit accounts, a banker's profits are made; but when we come to consider credit accounts, it is not so obvious to the non-professional.

It may be asked, What balance will pay a banker for keeping my account? To this very natural enquiry we can only reply by asking such questions as, What will be the extent of your transactions? how many cheques will you draw? shall you require either loans or discounts, and to what amount? Until these are answered, it will be utterly impossible to estimate what balance will be remunerative.

In consideration of this subject, it must be borne in mind that a certain portion of the balance standing to a customer's credit must be retained in the banker's hands to meet current demands; and, supposing the balance to be 1000*l*., at least 200*l*. of that sum must be unprofitable.

Added to this we must assume that some of the nominal balance will consist of ' uncleared effects,' i.e. cheques and bills for which the money has not been received. Although cheques and bills of exchange arrived at maturity when paid in with bank-notes and coin are all placed immediately to the customer's account, it is expected that the portion of the credit consisting of those documents, will not be drawn against until sufficient time shall have elapsed for them to be cleared; and a memorandum is usually inserted at the beginning of the ' pass book ' stating what time this operation will require, which will not exceed a few hours

where the cheques are payable in the same town
as that in which the receiving bank is situated;
if they have to be sent through the country,
Clearing-house, or the post, three or four days
should be allowed. Of course, notes and coin
may be drawn against immediately.

By some it has been said that, with money at less
than 2½ per cent., the expenses of banking will
leave no margin for profit; to refute such an as-
sertion it is only necessary to point to the usual
dividends of the joint-stock banks. It is generally
the case, that as money rises in value the balances
in the hands of bankers decrease, and *vice versá*;
so that the low rate of interest is compensated for
by the additional amount deposited; and it must
be noted that, with a high rate of interest prevail-
ing, the bad debts will increase, however cautious
the banker may be.

Country banks are not affected by the changes
in the money market to the same extent as those
in London, as the former seldom lend to their
customers at a lower rate than 5 per cent.; they
do not, on the other hand, often decrease the rate
of allowance on deposits below 2½ per cent. It is
only in the employment of their reserves that
they feel the difference; this, as with the London

banker, is balanced by the increase or diminution
of deposits.

It has been estimated that the banker is remu-
nerated if the average balance of an account is
sufficient to show a profit of sixpence on each
cheque drawn. Adopting this view for the moment, suppose a customer with an average balance of 500l. and money at 3 per cent., 100l.
must be retained to meet current demands,
leaving 400l. to be made use of for the purposes
of the bank; this, at the rate mentioned, would
give 12l., so that the customer would be entitled
to draw 480 cheques per annum without any
charge. We cannot think this to be a fair remuneration; and, should these views be generally
adopted, we believe the dividends received by
joint-stock bank shareholders would speedily fall
from the high rates at which they have so long
stood.

By the introduction of the joint-stock banking
system into London, great facilities for banking
were created for those whose means would not admit
of their keeping a balance large enough to meet the
views of the private bankers, by making a small
charge for commission where the average balance
was not remunerative. Interest was then for the

first time allowed on current accounts when the balance exceeded 200*l.*

Before leaving this branch of our subject, we would address a few general remarks, which may perhaps be useful, to the large and ever-increasing class who keep banking accounts. A banker is bound to know his customer's handwriting, and for that reason, on opening a new account, he takes his customer's signature in the book kept for the purpose, in order that, in cases of doubt, he may verify any document presented for payment.

We wish to urge the importance of adhering closely to one style of signature, as a great preventive to the success of forgeries; and to protest against the fallacy that an illegible handwriting is the most difficult to imitate; experience all goes to prove the reverse; the more distinct the writing the more obstacles does it present to the forger.

On the death of a customer, the bank, previous to parting with any balance standing to his credit at his death, will require the production of the probate of the will of the deceased for registration in the bank's books, after which the balance is at the disposal of the executors. Where the deceased died intestate, the ~~heir-at-law~~ must produce letters of administration.

the administrator

Enquiries as to the standing or means of any customer are *never* answered by bankers to private individuals; so that, to obtain information of the kind, the person requiring it is obliged to make use of his own banker. This precaution is a safeguard against malice and idle curiosity.

An order restraining bankers from parting with money is sometimes granted by the judges of the superior courts, and must be obeyed, at the risk of being committed for contempt of court.

There are various ways in which customers may save their bankers considerable time, without entailing any great trouble on themselves.

Bankers always furnish to their customers printed forms, called 'credit tickets,' which are divided into different heads, and should be filled up and taken to the bank with the cheques, &c.

All cheques and bills of exchange should be carefully examined, to see whether stamps or indorsements are required; in a word, whether they are regular.

Should a clerk or servant be sent for a cheque-book or any document belonging to a customer, it is necessary to have a written order for its delivery.

The only receipt usually given by bankers is the

acknowledgment by entry in the pass book; there are, however, some exceptions to this rule.

It is always advisable to cross cheques remitted by post, if the name of the payee's banker be known, with his name; if not, with the words 'and company.' Should the cheque be delivered to the payee, it is a good plan to ask for his banker's name, and cross it.

Besides bills of exchange, of which mention will be made in a future chapter, there are various securities on which advances will be readily made by bankers.

Securities transferable by delivery, such as exchequer bills and the bonds of colonial and foreign governments, are the most available; the possession being sufficient, it is only necessary for the borrower to give a lien to the banker, who will then advance according to the value of the securities for the time being, retaining a margin for eventualities.

Government stocks, as consols, &c., are required by bankers, previous to an advance, to be transferred from the name of the customer to that of some partner or officer of the bank; this only entails the trouble of making the transfer, as the consideration is merely nominal. Many bankers object to lend money on shares in railways or trading companies, for this reason — unless the shares are regularly transferred, the security is not tangible; and should the precaution of having a transfer executed be adopted, the lender makes himself liable for any calls the company make, and in the event of insolvency, for the debts incurred.

Dock warrants and bills of lading are frequently advanced on, but many bankers consider it an unsound practice.

Life-assurance policies are almost invariably objected to as security for advances, except as a ‘make-weight.’ The chief objections to be urged against them are, that the validity entirely depends on punctual payment of the premiums, and should the owner neglect such payments, the holder must in self-defence make it right, or his security is valueless. It is necessary that a life office should be informed of the assignment of any policies to any third person, otherwise, in case of death, there will probably be difficulty, if not litigation, before a settlement will be made.

When an advance is made by a banker on the title deeds of real property, it would appear to be sufficient that the borrower should write a letter stating the circumstances, and giving a lien on the property. It may, however, be safer to require an undertaking to execute a regular mortgage if called on to do so.

A banker has no right to detain, or appropriate to the payment of an overdrawn account, property of any description which has been placed in his hands for safe custody; it must be given up to the owner on his application, although he may be indebted to the banker at the time to the full amount of the property. Nor can a banker (without the express consent of his customer) appropriate any balance realised by the sale of securities, deposited to cover a specific advance, towards the liquidation of any claim that may have arisen since such deposit.

CHAPTER IV.

CHEQUES.

CHEQUES, which are such an important part of
the circulation of the country, appear to have
had their origin so far back as the times of the
Romans, though it is difficult to fix the exact
date of their introduction. The names by which
these documents were known were 'attributio'
and 'prescriptio.' We cannot discover that any
great use of them took place either in this country or abroad until about the year 1780, when
the bankers in London adopted them instead of
the goldsmiths' notes, of which they then discontinued the issue. Since that time the use of
cheques has extended year by year; and although
there do not exist any data by which either the

number or amount drawn may be arrived at, it must come to a total of some hundreds of millions per annum. A cheque is an order addressed to a banker by his customer to pay a sum of money on demand.

It is not necessary that a cheque to be legal should be couched in any particular form of words, although the banker, if he give due notice, may refuse to pay cheques not drawn according to his directions. The best plan is to adhere to the printed cheques, which all bankers now issue to their customers free of charge, as the use of plain paper does away with one difficulty for the forger —the obtaining possession of the blank cheque.

We believe it is now correct to say that all bankers issue printed cheques to their customers; it is, however, only within the last fifteen years that the custom has been adopted by the old-established firm of Child & Co. The place where a cheque is drawn ought to be truly stated, and the date must be that of the day on which it is issued.

Prior to 1853 all cheques were unstamped, and were illegal documents if dated more than fifteen miles from the bank on which they were drawn; in that year an Act was passed by which such

cheques were legalised, provided they bore either
an impressed or adhesive penny stamp, and the
drawers were allowed the privilege of making
these cheques payable to 'order' instead of to
'bearer,' the effect of which will be mentioned
below. This Act was constantly evaded by dating
the cheque from the town on which it was drawn;
it led, moreover, to endless disputes as to distance,
and finally was a failure as a source of revenue.
An Act which came into operation in 1858
obliged all cheques drawn by private individuals
to bear the penny stamp, with the exception of
those payable to 'self,' drawn at the bank counter,
or paid to an authorised person for the use of the
drawer.

This exception has been since abolished, and
at present the only cheques which are legal
unstamped are those of some of the Government offices, poor-law unions, and charities; the
transfers passing between bankers are likewise
exempted.

The stamp should be put on by the drawer, but
should he omit it, the payee, or any one who presents the cheque, can legalise it by affixing a
stamp. Cheques drawn out of the United Kingdom are considered by law as foreign bills, and

require to have 'ad valorem' foreign stamps.
The Channel Islands and the Isle of Man are
included in the word foreign.

Post-dated cheques, i.e. cheques bearing date
subsequent to the actual drawing, are illegal; the
drawer, payee, and the banker who knowingly
pays such cheques, incur penalties of 100l. in the
drawer and banker's case, and 20l. in that of the
payee.*

The reason of this is obvious, as post-dated
cheques if used may do away with the necessity
for bills of exchange, and thus defraud the revenue
of the stamp duty thereon.

The practice of crossing cheques, which is now
so general, is a most important safeguard against
fraud.

It originated with the Clearing-house, the clerks
of which used to cross the cheques they delivered to other bankers with the name of their
own house; and gradually the public adopted
the system. For many years, however, although
bankers used to act upon the crossing, it was not
compulsory to do so; and it appears, by decisions

* There seems to be some doubt whether a post-dated cheque, if
payable to 'order,' is invalid.—Byles on Bills, 8th edit. p. 16; Grant
on Banking, 2nd edit. p. 15.

in the law courts, that legally a banker was
obliged to pay a crossed cheque payable to bearer,
although presented at the counter by a private
individual.

In the year 1856 an Act was passed by which
bankers were compelled to refuse:—1. Cheques
crossed 'and Co.' if not presented through *a*
banker.   2. Cheques crossed with the name of a
banker, unless presented by that banker; and it
follows as a matter of course that cheques crossed
to two bankers must share the same fate.   By the
same Act the alteration or erasure of a crossing
is a forgery.

We have seen that by the Act of 1853 the
drawer is allowed to make a stamped cheque payable to 'order;' the effect of this is, that the
payee, before presenting it for payment or otherwise negotiating it, must indorse it in the same
way as a bill of exchange.

Should the drawer have made any mistake in
the orthography or style of the payee, this latter
must in indorsing copy the error; he can add the
correct name beneath.

Providing an indorsement agree with the filling
up of the cheque, the banker will pay it; and
should it afterwards appear that the indorsement

was a forgery, he will not be held responsible for not discovering it.

Bankers will pay cheques indorsed per procuration; although the legality of such practice was doubtful for a time, the most recent decisions establish it.

The payee of a cheque is bound to present it in 'reasonable time;' and according to late judgments it appears that the limit is the close of business hours on the day following the receipt of the cheque. If he holds it longer than this, he does it at his own risk, as to the insolvency of the banker as well as the drawer; also in case of the death of the latter, the banker would decline to pay the cheque.

Non-presentation of a cheque does not release the drawer from his liability, unless he has actually sustained loss from the holding of the cheque, which he would do in the following hypothetical case :

A gives a cheque on B to C, who feeling satisfied with the stability of A, does not present the cheque for several days, during which time B fails, having assets of A's in his hands. Here C holds the cheque at his own risk; had he presented it on receipt, or within a day or two, it would have been

paid. For A to bear the consequences of C's
neglect would be obviously unjust, for by the non-
presentation of the cheque his balance in B's
hands is larger than it would otherwise have been,
and his loss by the failure would be thus increased
by the amount of the cheque.

Had A's been an overdrawn account he would
not have been injured by C's conduct, the only
effect of which would be that A was indebted to
D's assignees to a lesser amount than he would
otherwise have been.

The holder of a cheque, not being the payee, is
bound to present it during business hours not
later than the day following its receipt; otherwise
he releases the person from whom he received it,
in the event of the insolvency of the bank or the
dishonour of the cheque.

For this holder (in case of insolvency of the
bank) to be able to charge the drawer, it is necessary that the cheque, whatever number of hands
it may have passed through, should be presented
in the same time as if it had remained in the
original payee's possession. Here, however, if the
drawer has received no injury from non-presentation, his liability is not cancelled.

Respecting a cheque drawn on a bank at a distance from the place where the payee resides, it would seem sufficient that the post of the second day should be the medium of presentation.

Bankers are bound to honour the cheques of their customers if the funds in their hands are sufficient, unless the time that has elapsed since the money was paid in, has been too short for the necessary entries to be made; in which case no action for damages would lie.

Should a banker after knowledge of an act of bankruptcy pay a customer's cheque, he is liable to an action by the assignees for the recovery of the amount.

A banker must not pay the cheque of a customer of whose death he has received intelligence. A banker would be justified in refusing to pay a cheque, although he may have funds sufficient, providing that those funds have been placed in his hands to meet specific claims, of which the cheque in point forms no part.

In the event of the dishonour of a cheque through the negligence of the banker, he would be liable to an action for damages to the drawer for the injury to his credit; but the payee or holder would have no remedy against the banker.

When a banker receives instructions from a

customer not to pay a particular cheque, he is held harmless. It should be mentioned, however, that the holder, if he has *bona fide* given value for it, can recover the whole amount from the drawer.

Bankers will not pay without enquiry cheques that have been long drawn; but no stated time seems to have been laid down beyond which they ought to refuse payment. It would therefore appear to be left to their discretion to act as the circumstances of each case seem to warrant. In practice a banker would write to his customer for instructions before paying a cheque dated more than twelve months previous to presentation.

A banker cannot debit his customer with a forged cheque, nor for one that has been fraudulently altered, unless the drawer by his way of filling it up has facilitated the alteration. The following case, taken from 'Byles on Bills,' p. 24, will best explain this:—

A customer of a banker on leaving home intrusted to his wife some blank cheques, signed by himself, to be used in the business when requisite. She filled up one with the words fifty-two pounds, two shillings, beginning the word fifty with a small letter in the middle of a line. The figures 52 : 2 were also placed at a considerable distance

to the right of the printed £. She gave the cheque
to her husband's clerk to get the money. He,
before presenting it, inserted the words 'three
hundred' before the word fifty, and the figure 3
between the printed £ and the figures 52 : 2. It·
was paid by the bankers for £352 2s. Held, that
the improper mode of filling up the cheque had
invited the forgery, and, therefore, that the loss
must fall on the customer and not on the banker.

A cheque is not a legal tender, and for that
reason may be objected to; but having been accepted by a creditor, he cannot proceed for his
debt until he has presented and been refused
payment for the cheque.

It is usual where a cheque has been taken in
payment of a bill of exchange not to part with
the bill, but to attach it to the cheque, so that the
drawer receives both together from his bankers.

The mere production of a cancelled cheque is
not sufficient evidence of the discharge of a debt;
it is necessary to prove that the cheque has actually
passed through the creditor's hands.

A cheque is not evidence of the loan of money
from the drawer to the payee; nor can a banker
produce cheques paid by him to prove an advance
to his customer.

It is the practice of London bankers to return the cheques and bills paid by them on behalf of their customers with the pass books in which the debits are entered. We believe that country bankers generally do not adopt this rule, but retain cheques, subject, of course, to inspection.

The law on the subject seems to be, that a paid cheque is the absolute property of the customer, by reason of his having paid for the stamp directly, and indirectly for the cheque, by the profit on his account. Now the law also says that a banker's books are not evidence in his favour, although they may be against him.

The paid cheque being returned, and the banker's books not evidence, the question may arise, how, in the event of a customer disputing the payment of a particular cheque, and alleging that all his paid vouchers had been destroyed, the banker would be able to rebut this statement, having already parted with both the order to pay and the receipt for the money?

CHAPTER V.

BILLS OF EXCHANGE.

The use of a Bill of Exchange—The form of drawing—Respecting alterations—Agreement of body with figures—Bills of Exchange drawn in sets—Presentation at maturity; before maturity; after maturity—Mode of proceeding with Dishonoured Bill—Notation of protest; necessity for, and security of—Acceptance; acceptance contrary to tenor—Stamps, Inland and foreign—Indorsements—Bankruptcy of acceptor—Statute of Limitations, as affecting Bills of Exchange—Payment—Cases in which a Banker is justified in refusing payment of a Bill or Note—Discounting Bills—Indications in case of need—The 'copy' of a Bill.

1. *The Use of a Bill of Exchange.*

A BILL of exchange was employed, in the first instance, simply as a letter of credit from one country to another, much more extensive in form than the document used in the present day, and containing an amount of matter which time has gradually reduced to its present more business-like dimensions. This mode of settling accounts between merchants in distant lands, was found to be of infinite use, as it obviated the great risk of

H

carrying large amounts of specie, and told at a
glance the value of the document, thereby considerably facilitating pecuniary transactions in
commercial intercourse. These bills of exchange,
after having done duty from one country to another, changed hands frequently before they were
finally disposed of.

Bills of exchange, on being introduced into this
country, were discovered to be of greater use
than merely as the representatives of so much
money, as they could be instrumental in effecting
the assignment of a debt, and as such are now
recognised by the common law. Not only was the
debt transferred, but its value was enhanced, inasmuch as the debtor himself accepted to pay
a *certain* amount, from which engagement he
could not afterwards depart. These bills of exchange were allowed only among merchants at
first; but, as commerce increased, they became
common with all classes of traders. In the present
day, the extent to which bills of exchange are
used may be conceived from the fact of their being
by far the most important documents employed in
commerce, many hundreds of millions sterling
being circulated annually in this country in the
form of bills of exchange.

2. *The Form of Drawing.*

In drawing a bill or note the law does not compel the maker to use ink; the document would have the same effect if written in pencil; but the liability to obliteration would prevent the use of a pencil, except in cases where no other material was at hand. There are usually three parties to a bill of exchange: 1st, the drawer; 2nd, the drawee, who, on the completion of the document, becomes acceptor; and 3rd, the payee—the person to whom the amount specified in the bill or note is to be paid, to his order or to the bearer, as the case may be. Frequently, the drawer is also the payee. When the payee's name is followed by the word 'order'—which is the most customary method—an indorsement becomes necessary previous to the instrument changing hands. The word 'bearer' coming after the payee's name, renders any writing unnecessary in the event of transfer—'bearer' simply implying anybody. It is very unusual to draw a bill of exchange payable to 'bearer,' although no legal objection can be raised against it.* It is scarcely necessary to

* In case Rex *v.* Randall, Eyre, C.B., ruled that a bill payable to blank or order was waste paper. In Minet *v.* Gibson, the majority of the judges held an opposite opinion.

explain that the 'holder' of a bill is the person in actual—or, as Sir J. B. Byles says, in 'constructive'—possession, and legally entitled to recover the amount specified, from the parties thereto.

Inland bills of exchange are drawn on demand, at so many days', or weeks', or months', sight or date, as the case may require, or payable on such a day named therein; in all cases, excepting with the paper of the Bank of England, carrying three days' grace. Where no time is named, the document is payable on demand.

Foreign bills are the same in form as inland bills, but they will sometimes be drawn at longer dates, according to the distance of the countries from one another, between which they are to operate; the tenor, however, depends upon a variety of circumstances, and may be extended to almost any period, provided the parties thereto are agreed. It will stand to reason that the longer a bill has to run the less will its value be, and the more difficult its negotiation.

A note drawn payable by instalments is held good, and the holder is protected by the statute 3 & 4 Queen Anne; three days of grace may be demanded for every instalment. The term 'usance,' in connection with foreign bills, denotes the customary tenor at which bills are drawn, depending upon the distance between countries; where 'usance' is half a month, the time is fifteen days.

A 'sola' bill of exchange is a single bill, as distinguished from bills drawn in 'sets.' In drawing a bill of exchange, care should be taken in the description of the payee, that he be not confounded with another of similar name. When a bill is drawn by procuration, the authority to draw is admitted, but not to indorse. If a bill miscarry—unless payable to 'bearer'—the unlawful possessor can neither acquire nor convey any title thereto.

The power given to another person to draw, accept, or indorse, by the term 'per procuration,' is recognised by the law only to a limited extent. It is held that any person giving value for a *bill* drawn, indorsed, or accepted 'per procuration,' without inquiring as to what extent such authority has been given, does so at his own risk, and will lose the amount if the authority be unauthorised. With cheques, however, the contrary has been maintained, and we are of opinion with justice. In the despatch of business it is quite impossible for a banker to ascertain the genuineness of a 'per procuration' indorsement upon a cheque, without causing unreasonable delay; in addition to which, the banker should not be made to suffer for the negligence of others, or be compelled to take the responsibility of the risk, which other people must run, of engaging dishonest and untrustworthy persons to assist them with their business. In all such cases great care should be taken to define the extent of the authority given, as, permission having occasionally been given to indorse, a jury might consider themselves justified in inferring that the authority was general. A bill drawn to the order of one person and indorsed by another of similar name, is held to be a forgery. Promissory notes drawn upon forms having printed dates, and payable to bearer on demand, are subject to a penalty of 50l. In drawing a bill, it is better, although not absolutely necessary, to state the amount in figures as well as in writing. If the body and figures differ, the body will be taken to be the amount for which the bill is made payable. A bill may be drawn at any tenor without objection. Drawing a bill after so many days' sight, literally means after legal acceptance, and must not be taken to mean a mere exhibition of the document to the drawee. When a bill is drawn at so many months' sight or date, the month must be understood to be calendar. A bill drawn at so many days' sight, must be computed exclusively of the day on which it is sighted, and inclusively of the day it falls due. A bill drawn, indorsed, or accepted in blank by an infant, does not bind him, if it be filled up after he is of age.

The 'grace' allowed upon bills varies considerably in different countries. Three days are allowed in England, Scotland, Ireland, North America, Vienna, Bergamo, and Berlin. At St. Petersburg, ten days on bills drawn after date, and on bills presented after they are due; three days on sight bills. Parts of Brazil, Bahia, and Rio, fifteen days. Frankfort four days. Leipsic, Naumburg, and Augsburg, five days. Cologne, Breslau, Nuremburg, Portugal, Antwerp, Venice, Amsterdam, Rotterdam, Middleburg, Königsberg, and Duntzic, ten days.* Hamburgh three days, of which the day the bill falls due is one. At Stockholm there are no days of grace, but it is customary not to protest until the day after the due date. The above periods of grace said to be allowed by some foreign countries will be found to be the exception and not the rule, where the number of days exceeds two or three, as such long periods of grace are associated with obsolete systems which have

---

* Days of grace are abolished altogether in France.

gradually disappeared as the principles of political economy have become better understood.

It is not customary to allow grace on bills drawn ' at sight,' although the legality is still a disputed point. Bills or notes on demand carry no grace; an instrument made payable on demand is rightly termed a draft. It must be remembered that in computing bills drawn in Russia or Turkey, in consequence of their adherence to the old style, twelve days must be allowed. It is held that a bill or note, neither payable to order nor bearer, is *not* a negotiable instrument, though it remains valid as a security between the original parties.

In drawing a bill the employment of the words ' value received' are not—as supposed by many— essential parts of a bill, as made between drawer and acceptor, or between drawer and payee. Without the drawer's signature, a bill, even if it be accepted, is useless. Although custom demands it, the law does not compel the drawer to sign in any particular part of the document. A person unable to write may sign by his mark properly witnessed. If the drawer of a bill attach his signature to a blank form, he is responsible and liable for anything that may be filled in after, within the amount carried by the stamp. In case of a bill of exchange being dishonoured, and an action brought against the drawer, he cannot be proceeded against if he can prove that the document was not presented at the place where the drawee had originally accepted it payable. Direction as to where payable may be made in any part of the bill, provided the acceptance be appended. In the case of a promissory note, this is not applicable, for if the place of payment be noticed merely in a disconnected part of the document, in the form of a memorandum, it has been held to be a fatal misdescription ; it should be stated in the body, and thereby become part of the contract. Where an instrument is drawn in a careless way, in the form of a promissory note, and accepted, and indorsed as a bill of exchange, the holder may treat it as either, at his option. A bill made payable to the order of the drawee, it is hardly necessary to state, is not a bill of exchange. An instrument instructing the drawee to pay without accepting, is a legal bill of exchange.

Bills and notes demand payment in specie or Bank of England notes only; other descriptions of goods are not considered payment, and if drawn to include other than specie payment, are invalid. If drawn subject to additions or deductions of

interest, the document is of no use, even for
the original amount.   Bills or notes, the payment
of which depend on any uncertain event, such as
marriage, or the realisation of sums of money
consequent upon any speculation, are not coun-
tenanced by the law, and are useless as evidence.
In case of a memorandum being added after the
completion and handing over of the document, by
way of defeasance, it is looked upon as a separate
and independent agreement, and must have a
proper stamp; but it must be remembered that an
agreement must be only between the original
parties to the instrument, and that any collateral
arrangement will be of no avail as regards an
interference with the progress of the bill or note.
Any oral agreement is useless against a written
contract.

3. *Respecting alterations.*

A bill of exchange or note ceases to be of any
value after having been altered in a material part,
irrespective of who may have made such alteration.
Persons holding such documents are considered
bound in obedience to the laws of society to uphold
them in their integrity both as regards their own
acts and those of other people who may in the

course of business hold such instruments in their hands for the account of their employers.

An alteration made by the drawer or other holder, without the consent or knowledge of the acceptor, is considered a full discharge to the acceptor. The acceptor pledges himself to pay at a certain place; any alteration of that, without his knowledge, releases him from his original contract. A person indorsing a bill so altered to another person ignorant of the alteration, cannot sue his indorser upon default; the acceptor not being held responsible for a change from the place where he had undertaken to pay. Any alteration made with the consent of an acceptor does not invalidate the instrument, but an alteration made in a material part of the document upsets it under the Stamp Act, as by such alteration it becomes a new instrument requiring a new stamp. Material alterations are—in the date, tenor, sum, making negotiable an instrument which before was not so; altering the words 'value received,' so as to mean any other consideration—all these avoid the bill under the Stamp Act. An alteration before the delivery of the instrument will not vitiate it; nor will the alteration of any slight error which may have occurred by which the original intention of the maker is furthered. Either payee or indorsee having given value for the bill, an alteration, though *before* acceptance, avoids the document. An alteration made at any period by the drawer or payee, though it renders void the instrument, does not extinguish the debt. An alteration by an indorsee not only liberates all the antecedent parties, but extinguishes the debt due to the indorsee by the indorser. The renewal of a bill consequent on any alteration, does not render liable parties to the original, unless duly apprised thereof.

4. *Agreement of Body with Figures.*

In cases of difference between body and figures, it is held that the writing in the body—being, in fact, the principal substance of the instrument—should be presumed to be the amount intended, as it is more probable that an error would occur in the figures. A banker having a bill presented thus differing, and holding no advice—which is frequently the case—would be governed in his actions by the nature of the alteration.

5. *Bills of Exchange drawn in Sets.*

In purchasing bills of exchange in one country to remit to another, it is customary to draw two or three bills to a set; but more must be furnished if demanded. In most cases, only two are required. However many bills may be drawn in a set, they compose but one bill. All the parts of a set must be numbered alike, so that each has undoubted reference to the other part. Each of such parts contains the written condition that it will be paid, provided only that no other part of the same bill has been already paid. The mode of dealing with the parts may differ, according to circumstances. A purchaser may not intend to employ the 'second' at all, but only to hold it in case the 'first' should be lost, in which event the 'second' answers his purpose as well as the 'first.' The 'first' may be forwarded for acceptance, and the 'second' indorsed away for value, subsequently finding its way to the accepted 'first,' to which it will be attached, and both paid at maturity. The payment of any one part extinguishes the whole. The parts of a bill not being written so as to show undoubted reference one to the other, may oblige the drawer to pay more than one part in the event of anything going wrong. A drawee will, of course, take care to accept only one part, and always to obtain possession by payment of such part as he may have accepted, otherwise he may have to pay twice.

6. Presentation at Maturity—Before Maturity— After Maturity.

It is not necessary, on the arrival of a bill at maturity, to present it to the acceptor personally. It is his business to provide for it at the place indicated. It is absolutely necessary that the bill or note should be presented, when due, at the place indicated, otherwise legal proceedings will be of no avail against the indorsers. The acceptor or maker, however, still remains liable; but a person who guarantees the payment of a bill is *not* released by the non-presentment. A reasonable time is allowed to present a bill payable on demand. If it be received one day, it is not necessary that it should be presented until the day after. A promissory note, payable on demand, may be taken as an exception to this rule, as it is frequently given as a continuing security, carrying interest. It is not, therefore, considered sufficient neglect to discharge the indorser, if it be presented within

a reasonable time after its reception. Where bills
are made payable at private houses, with no recognised hours of business (such as bankers have), as
late as eight o'clock in the evening is not considered unreasonable by the law. If a bill be
drawn, payable at a certain place, even though it
be different from that indicated by the acceptance, presentment must be made there, in order
to charge the drawer. If a bill be made payable at one of two places, presentment at either
will suffice. Proof of presentment at the place
indicated, though no one were in attendance,
neither did the acceptor live there, would suffice.
In the case of a promissory note, the place of
payment must be mentioned in the body of the
document, so as to be a part of the contract.
Presentment at a place indicated in a detached
memorandum will not suffice, and is held to be
fatal to the document. Circumstances, however,
may exist in which non-presentment, when due,
will not discharge the antecedent parties—a bill
seized under an extent, for instance, as laches
cannot be imputed to the crown. Neglect to present, when due, discharges the antecedent parties
—the only recourse being against drawer and
acceptor. Should the acceptor, however, have

failed since the day of maturity, the drawer is also
released, unless the holder can satisfactorily prove
that, had the bill been presented at maturity, it
would have been refused for a sufficient reason,
such as no effects, no orders, nor advice.

7. *Mode of Proceeding with Dishonoured Bill.*

In case a bill should not be paid when presented,
it is customary and necessary to leave a written
notice, containing the particulars of the bill, so
that at a later period of the day the acceptor may
procure the funds necessary to meet the bill, and
prevent its being protested. Notice of dishonour
may be given by the holder's agent or attorney,
and in his own name stands good. Notice of dishonour should be given to each indorser, each
being entitled. The drawer of a bill, when payable
to a third party, is entitled to notice. Neither
the drawee nor acceptor of a bill, nor the maker
of a promissory note, is entitled to notice. It is
safest for the holder to give notice himself to all
the indorsers; as, if he only give notice to his
immediate indorser, and it is not regularly trans-
mitted to the antecedent parties, they are discharged. It is also necessary that there be no
laches in the circulation of the notices, no more

than one day being allowod between each, as any
neglect on the part of one indorser is not compensated for by extra diligence on the part of
another. Laches committed by any indorser discharges all the antecedent parties. If the party
be dead, notice must be given to his personal
representatives. Where a firm or number of people
are jointly liable on a bill, notice to one is sufficient. Notice of dishonour need not be given
when a bill is drawn on an insufficient stamp, nor
is it necessary to the indorser of a promissory note
not negotiable. A promise of part payment, or an
acknowledgment of liability, will be evidence of
notice.

8. *Notation of Protest—Necessity for, and Security of.*

Noting bills of exchange and promissory notes,
as is customary among bankers and merchants at
the present time, is a different operation from the
'notation of protest,' as regards foreign bills of
exchange. The mere 'noting' is a minute made
by the notary, an officer appointed by the Arch-
bishop of Canterbury, and whose appointment is
registered and subscribed by the Clerk of Her
Majesty for Faculties in Chancery.* Noting is

* The first instance of a woman being appointed as a 'Notary
public' occurred lately at Chicasaw County, Iowa.

I

recognised by the law as the preliminary step to
the protest, and is, strictly, a part of it. At the
same time, bills are noted when no protest is
intended. In a case of legal proceedings against
parties to a dishonoured bill, the notary would be
considered an essential witness of the presentment
and dishonour. The minute of the notary, which
is attached to the bill, is satisfactory evidence of
the document having been duly presented, either
for payment or acceptance. The notary is a person
conversant with such transactions, and is considered a qualified person to direct the holder as to
the course to be pursued. With respect to the
charges, it appears that, according to the resolu-
tions passed at a meeting of some of the notaries
belonging to the city of London, which was held
at the George and Vulture Tavern, on July 1, 1797,
the following charges were agreed to, which were
approved by the Bank of England:—For bills payable or to be accepted by persons living within
the old walls of London, 1s. 6d.; beyond the old
walls, and not farther than certain boundaries
known to the notaries, which it is scarcely needful
to specify at length, 2s. 6d.; beyond such boundaries, and not off the pavement, 3s. 6d.; every mile
after leaving the pavement, 1s. 6d. additional.

Bills protested within the old walls of the city of London, inclusive of a 4s. stamp-duty, and exclusive of noting charge, 6s. 6d.; without the old city walls, under the same conditions, 8s.

For all acts of honour within the walls upon any one bill, 1s. 6d.; without the walls, according to the charges before mentioned for bills which will cause the notary to proceed beyond the boundary of the old walls of the city of London.

It was not allowed by the law to recover the notarial charges against the acceptor unless special damage was made in the declaration; but under an Act, 18 & 19 Vict., the expenses of noting may be recovered. The protest of a foreign bill is begun the day it falls due; but such custom does not exist everywhere, as in many countries no steps are taken at all until the evening of the second day, which is sufficient to protect the holder. All inland bills are not protested until the second day, or the day after the bill falls due. The protestation of foreign bills is customary among nations, as regulating international transactions. It affords undoubted proof of dishonour to the drawer, without which evidence he would have to rely upon the representation of the holder. The acts of a public functionary are credited by foreign Courts, and a bill protested under the seal of a foreign notary will be received as evidence in our courts of the dishonour of a bill payable abroad.

A foreign promissory note need not be protested.

In the absence of a notary-public, a protest may be made by any inhabitant of the place in the presence of two witnesses.

The form of a protest is a solemn declaration made under a fair copy of the bill, stating that payment or acceptance has been refused; assigning the reasons, if any, and that it is therefore protested.

A bill also may be protested for better security. Where the acceptor becomes insolvent, and his credit is publicly impeached before the bill falls due, the holder may employ a notary to demand better security, and, on refusal, the bill may be protested, and notice may be sent to an antecedent party; but no proceedings can be taken until after the bill has fallen due. A second acceptance may appear upon a bill for honour, but *not* without the intervention of a protest. Her Majesty's consuls residing abroad are empowered to do all notarial acts; also attorneys residing more than ten miles from the Royal Exchange may be admitted to practice as notaries. On occasions when a bill is refused acceptance, or is protested for better security, any person may accept for honour 'supra protest,' the form of which is as follows:—The acceptor, 'supra protest,' must appear personally with a witness before a notary-public, and declare that he accepts the bill for the honour of drawer or indorser, and that he will meet it at the appointed time, when he has to accept the bill 'supra protest' in the usual way in favour of whoever the person may be. When the acceptance 'supra protest' is made without mentioning the name, it is considered as made for the honour of the drawer.

9. *Acceptance.*

The literal meaning of the word acceptance, as applied to bills of exchange, signifies an engagement on the part of the drawee to meet the bill in money when it falls due; which engagement generally appears across the face of the instrument. But a bill of exchange may exist without an acceptance. An instrument drawn by A. upon B. directing him to pay C. a certain sum at a given time, without acceptance, is a bill of exchange. A bill must be accepted by the intended drawee, except for honour. A partner by accepting binds his co-partners. A retired partner is only liable on those bills signed while he remained a partner. If a bill be drawn on several persons not in partnership, all must sign; if not, it may be treated as dishonoured; but acceptance will be binding on those who have accepted.

If any person be rash enough to accept on a blank form, he is liable for any amount which the stamp will cover. A written or oral promise to pay or accept an existing foreign bill, is considered at common law an acceptance. The holder of a bill must not agree to a qualified acceptance without giving notice to the previous parties; if such a proceeding takes place without their consent, they are discharged; but the holder must neither protest nor give notice of dishonour, as he thereby precludes himself from recovering against the acceptor.

Acceptances may be made conditionally; such, for instance, as an agreement to pay the bill when certain monies were realised. A bill accepted for a part of the sum for which it was drawn is held good, and may be sued on *pro tanto*. The acceptance of a bill by the drawee may be cancelled at any time, provided the bill has not been delivered or the fact of acceptance been made known to the holder. The cancellation of an acceptance by the acceptor's banker does not render the banker legally liable, if it can be proved that due care was taken. The cancellation of the acceptor's name by the holder is equivalent to a discharge. The acceptor of a bill, when it has once been delivered, is supposed to have satisfied himself that all is right, and cannot withdraw on the plea of the drawer's signature being forged; he also admits the capacity of the payee to indorse, and cannot set up the infancy of the payee, or the fact of the drawer being a married woman, as a plea.

Care should be taken also as regards a bill, being drawn by a married woman, as the husband can sue or indorse; the consequence of which may be that the acceptor will be compelled to pay the bill twice.

If an acceptor die before the maturity of a bill, it must still be presented for payment; if necessary, demand must be made at the executor's place of abode, and, on refusal, must be protested.

10. *Acceptance contrary to Tenor.*

A bill may be protested for acceptance contrary to tenor; that is, if it be accepted for a longer

date than is mentioned in the bill. Acceptance
may, however, be taken, whichever way the
drawee accepts, as a second protest may be made
for non-payment at the expiration of the time mentioned in the bill. No one can discharge the acceptor of a bill except the holder or some one
authorised by him.

11. Stamps—Inland and Foreign.

It will be unnecessary here to go into the origin
of stamps, and the changes that have taken place,
as they have from time to time appeared on bills
of exchange and promissory notes; suffice it to
explain the custom of the present time. It may,
perhaps, be advisable to state that stamps were
first brought into use in the year 1782. Bills
drawn for the expenses of the army and navy, or for
the transfer of money from one bank to another,
require no stamps. Inland bills of exchange are
subject to an *ad valorem* duty, denoted by impressed stamps. The tenor of a bill does not affect
the stamp duty, except when payable on demand,
then the bill requires a penny stamp irrespective
of the amount for which it is drawn. Foreign
bills or notes, whether payable on demand or otherwise, are subject to an *ad valorem* duty denoted

by·adhesive stamps. A bill not duly stamped is no evidence in law or equity; but it cannot be held as a defence, in case of forgery, that the instrument was unduly stamped. A bill or note drawn to carry interest does not necessitate the employment of a higher stamp than was required for the amount actually specified at the commencement, although interest be received from a day prior to the date of the instrument. A bill or note bearing a stamp of greater value than is necessary (if of the proper denomination) is valid. It is necessary that all unimpressed stamps should be cancelled by the date, and the initials of the person affixing them. A promissory note which amounts to a mortgage, may be impressed with the mortgage stamp after it is made.

12. *Indorsements.*

An indorsement should always appear at the back of the instrument. Payment of a bill or note, however, need not bo refused on account of the indorsement appearing on the face, as it has the same effect legally. An indorsement is a conditional contract on the part of the indorser to pay the immediate or any succeeding indorsee, in case of the acceptor's or maker's default. On indorsing a bill or note to another person, care should be taken to spell the indorsee's name correctly, as much unnecessary delay occurs in business for want of this precaution, it being presumed that it is not the person intended when the spelling of the name differs. The mis-spelling of an indorsement does not necessarily avoid the instrument. A payee indorsing a bill not negotiable is liable to his indorsee; for each indorser takes the place as it were of a new drawer. It seems, however, that the bill not being negotiable, destroys the stamp, and the indorsee cannot acquire a right without a new stamp, which is contrary to law. The indorsement of a note—whether negotiable or not—by a person to whom it has not been transferred, does not render him liable on his indorsement; for though each indorser of a bill may be treated as a new drawer or maker, and in that capacity requires notice of dishonour, yet the indorser of a note cannot, without altering his situation for the worse, be treated as the drawer or maker of the *note*, as he thereby loses his right to notice of dishonour. A bill payable to order cannot be transferred without indorsement. An indorsement may be either special or

blank; the former is when the indorser indorses
the instrument to another person, who must affix
his signature if it be intended further to nego-
tiate it, or to receive the contents at maturity;
the latter, when the indorser merely signs his
name, after which it is payable to bearer. No
particular form of words is necessary to constitute an indorsement. If the number of indorsements exceed the limit of paper an additional
slip may be attached, which becomes part of the
instrument, and requires no further stamp. The
French call this additional slip an *allonge*. If
two persons are made payees of a bill, not being
partners, they must both indorse. Neither an
indorsement nor an acceptance is complete before
delivery; giving in charge to a servant would
not be considered a legal transfer of the property,
but to a postman it would. It has been held
that if there be a written, or even verbal agreement between a first indorser and his immediate
indorsee, that the indorsee shall not sue the indorser, but the acceptor only, it would be a good
defence on the part of the indorser in the event
of such agreement being broken; it would be
unadvisable however, under any circumstances,
to have only parole evidence of such an agree-

ment. A transfer by indorsement gives a right of
action to the indorsee against all persons whose
names appear on the bill, in case of default of
acceptance or payment. If a payee transfer a bill
without indorsing, the holder has no remedy in
his own name against any one, but the person
from whom he received it; but if it can be shown
that the bill was delivered purposely without
being indorsed, when it was intended that it
should be indorsed, an action may be maintained
against the indorsee or his personal representatives by a bill in equity, to obtain indorsement.
A person making a trustee the depository of a
bill of exchange to be used for certain purposes,
should show in the indorsement to what purpose
it was to be applied, which is termed a 'restrictive indorsement.' The transferer of a bill payable to bearer, and consequently without indorsement, does not become liable in the event of the
instrument being dishonoured, as it is held to
be a *bond fide* sale *primd facie*, carrying no
evidence of antecedent parties. All documents
payable to bearer circulate as cash. An indorsement may be made before the bill is drawn, in
which case the indorser renders himself liable
for any amount within the stamp. A promissory

note, payable on demand, is not considered overdue, nor can any interest be recovered on it
unless there is some evidence upon it of its
having been presented and refused payment. As
we have before stated, it may be indorsed from
hand to hand as a continuing security. It is
held that if a bill be paid before it is due, it may
be indorsed over, and remain a valid security in
the hands of a *bond fide* indorsee, but a bill paid
at maturity cannot be reissued. The payment of
a bill before it is due does not extinguish it, any
more than if it were discounted. In case of
partial payment at maturity, the holder cannot
recover more than the balance of the acceptor.
A bill or note cannot be indorsed for part of
the sum remaining due to the indorser upon it,
as it would cause a plurality of actions against
prior parties, and would be contrary to the
custom of bankers and merchants; but if a bill
or note be indorsed, or delivered for a part of
the sum due upon it, and the limit is not specified on the instrument, the transferee is entitled
to sue the maker or acceptor for the whole
amount, and becomes the trustee of the transferer for the surplus. If a bill has been paid
in part for the acceptor, or drawer by an agent,

it may be indorsed for the remainder due. A
release at maturity is the same as payment at
maturity, and extinguishes the bill; but a premature release of a party liable on the bill, does
not discharge the releasee as against an indorsee
for value without notice. Where a holder has
died, having only signed his name, without delivery, his executor cannot complete the indorsement by delivery. A married woman acquiring
a right to a bill or note, either before or during
marriage, the husband should indorse. The
indorser of a note places himself in the position
of a surety to the maker, and thereby renders
himself liable in case the maker cannot pay.
An indorser of a bill not negotiable, renders
himself liable to be sued by his indorsee, the
indorser being the new drawer, and by his act
having deprived his indorsee of the right to sue
the acceptor or maker. An indorser may, however, enter into an agreement with his indorsee
not to hold him liable, in which case the indorsee
cannot sue; but a subsequent indorsee, unless
having had due notice of the agreement, may
sue. The holder of a bill cancelling an indorsement intentionally, discharges the indorser. A
person having twice indorsed the same bill, can-

not, as a rule, sue the intermediate indorsers. If a man commit a breach of trust by indorsing to a third person a bill indorsed to him for a particular purpose, the indorsee, cognizant of the breach of trust, cannot sue the real owner of the bill; but, on the contrary, the owner may bring an action to have the bill restored. A person taking an overdue bill renders himself liable to anything that may happen in connection with the bill; being overdue it is said to come ‘disgraced’ to the indorsee. A drawer or indorser taking up a bill at maturity, may, by indorsing it to another person, transfer the right to sue on the bill. The person having possession of a note, part of which has been already paid, can only indorse for the balance,

Indorsement by executors or administrators answers the same purpose as an indorsement by the deceased.

13. *Bankruptcy of Acceptor.*

When an acceptor becomes bankrupt, the holder can claim a dividend under the commission; for, on being made bankrupt, the acceptor is discharged by the law. Upon the same principle, the acceptor, being discharged at the suit of the indorsee, under the Insolvent Act, the indorsee has his remedy against the drawer. Where the holder agrees to a composition, the indorsers are discharged.

14. *Statute of Limitation as affecting Bills of Exchange.*

The Statute of Limitation does not destroy the debt, but only bars the remedy. The period beyond which no action can be brought is six years. As regards bills of exchange, the limitation dates from the time the bill falls due. When a bill is on demand, it is supposed to be payable immediately; therefore, the statute runs from the date of the instrument. If the person against whom an action was brought were beyond the reach of the law—as, for instance, an infant, a person imprisoned, or out of the country, &c.—the Statute of Limitation would date from the time such person became amenable to the law. A foreign statute of limitations is no defence in an English court in an action on a foreign contract, as the statute affects the remedy and not the construction of the contract. When the holder of a bill has allowed the Statute of Limitation to run out, and transfers it, the transferee is debarred from bringing an action; for he, being the trans-

feree of an overdue bill, stands in no better position
than the transferer. When a bill is made payable
by instalments, in case of default of any one instalment, the statute dates from the first default
against the whole amount. An action brought by
an administrator on a bill would commence from
the date the letters of administration were granted,
and not from the time when the bill fell due. A
note (say thirty days after sight) is not open to an
action until the expiration of that period after the
exhibition to the maker; but on a 'demand' note
the statute would run from the date of the instrument, in the same way as with a bill.

It must be remembered that an acknowledgment
will bar the Statute of Limitations; that is to say,
the six years begin to run from the date of such
acknowledgment.

15. *Payment.*

Payment must be made to the rightful holder,
as payment to any other person does not discharge
the acceptor. In the case of a banker crediting
his customer with an immature bill, which on its
arrival at maturity is dishonoured and not returned to the customer, the banker renders himself
liable for the sum, as he not only credited his client

with the amount, but gave him to understand that
it was paid. There are, however, instances in
which payment to a wrongful holder is protected;
where, for example, a bill or note is made payable
to bearer, or becomes so by an indorsement in
blank, a *bond fide* holder may demand payment,
and the payment is protected, provided there are
no indications of carelessness on the part of the
banker, and no circumstances to arouse suspicion;
for the law, as a general rule, decrees that, when
one of two innocent persons suffers at the hands of
a third, the one causing the loss must sustain it.
As regards bills of exchange and notes, the law in
respect of forged indorsements steps in in favour
of the public, and with cheques in favour of the
banker. A bill or note, not payable to bearer, but
transferable by indorsement — a transfer taking
place by forged indorsement, the payer is liable.
A bill is not finally discharged until paid by, or on
behalf of the acceptor; and a note by, or on behalf
of the maker. It was held formerly that part
payment by the drawer was a partial discharge to
the acceptor, but it is now decided that payment
by the drawer is no plea, but simply converts the
holder into a trustee for the drawer, when the
holder afterwards recovers of the acceptor. Pay-

ment by the drawer of an accommodation bill is a
complete discharge. A bill made payable by the
acceptor at his bankers, and taken up by a stranger,
the stranger thereby obtaining possession, is not a
payment by the acceptor. A bill paid before it is
due, and afterwards negotiated by a *bonâ fide* indorsement, is a valid security. It is held that
payment of a bill before it is due does not extinguish, as regards the antecedent parties, any more
than if it were discounted, as the difficulty of
ascertaining whether an anticipated payment had
been made would considerably interfere with the
circulation of bills and notes. The payer of a bill
can demand its delivery to him; if not paid, the
holder should keep possession. An agent, however,
is justified, according to accepted practice, in de-
livering up the bill on receipt of a cheque, even
though the cheque be dishonoured. The drawers
or indorsers in such a case would be discharged,
they having the right to insist on the delivery of
the bill into their hands on payment being made
by them. The customary practice among bankers
is, on receipt of a cheque in payment, to attach it
to the bill, so that, in case the cheque is dishonoured,
the banker retains possession of the bill. Credit
given to the holder of a bill by the person ultimately

liable is considered equivalent to payment. When
a banker makes advances on a promissory note
received from a customer and his surety to cover a
running balance, the note is not discharged by
sums subsequently repaid and not appropriated to
the discharge of the note, but it still continues as
a security for the existing balance. A receipt on
the back of a bill is *primâ facie* evidence of payment by the acceptor; and, on paying a bill, a
receipt can be demanded, and should always be
taken. If a drawee discover on the same day that
payment was made, that the bill or note was a
forgery, he can, as a rule, recover the money. If
a bill be paid with the understanding that the
payer is to have possession of the instrument, and
it is afterwards withheld, an action may be brought
to retract the payment; also, an indorser may sue
if he has been induced by fraud to pay a bill on
behalf of the person liable. Care should be taken
in paying bills to see that all is right previous to
cancellation, as this is considered to extinguish
the instrument. The payment of a bill to a person
declared a bankrupt is unsafe, inasmuch as the
bankrupt's property vests in the assignees, from
whom alone a valid discharge can be obtained. If
partial payment has been received from the acceptor

at maturity, the holder can recover only the balance. Payment of a lost bill may be obtained by giving a satisfactory indemnity to the court. A renewal bill being dishonoured, an action may be brought on the original.

16. *Cases in which a Banker is justified in refusing payment of a Bill or Note.*

On being presented with a bill for payment, the first thing a banker looks to is to ascertain if he holds sufficient funds, without which, it is hardly necessary to state, the document must be dishonoured. It is more prudent in all cases to give a banker advice of bills becoming due, without which, any informalities, &c., might give rise to suspicion, and cause injurious delay, perhaps refusal. In cases, however, where a customer is particular in providing for the proper payment of his acceptances, the banker will use his own discretion as to the refusal, as the consequences may be very serious from dishonouring a bill of exchange on account of trivial irregularities. A bill of exchange being refused, for instance, in consequence of an erroneous computation as to the due date on the part of the banker—there being sufficient funds to meet the bill, and before the represent-

ment of the bill the funds disappeared — the
banker would most likely suffer in case the other
parties to the instrument were to take advantage
of the banker's negligence.   Such an oversight
would in all probability be speedily remedied
without such loss to the banker; at the same
time a banker renders himself liable in the same
way by non-payment as by non-presentment.   An
insufficient stamp, as we have previously stated,
makes the document illegal, and it must therefore
be refused payment on that ground.   Irregularity
of indorsement — difference between body and
figures, erasure of any vital part of the bill, any
apparently subsequent addition made after acceptance to alter the purport of the instrument, an
alteration of date so as to prolong the period the
bill had to run, or to shorten it — would justify
the banker in refusing payment, unless satisfactory explanation were offered on which he
could act with safety to himself and for the welfare of his customer.

17. *Discounting Bills.*

Discounting bills—that is, placing the amount
which the bills represent to the customer's credit,
minus the interest — is a very common custom

among bankers, and is of itself a business with
some, who style themselves 'bill discounters.'*
Firms trading largely on a small capital find discounting a great assistance, and in some cases
are unable to do without it; but bankers are
always cautious to ascertain that the paper is of
a good class, or moderately so, before they discount to any great extent; as when the accommodation afforded is to a person of but limited
capital, in the event of an adverse crisis the
banker will probably suffer. Discounting, however, is not confined to trading firms solely, but
is considerably resorted to by money-lenders, and
all kinds of people who can lend their money
at a higher rate of interest than they pay for it.
It must be remembered, however, that a discounted bill should never be delivered to any one
but the depositor of it until after maturity; as
not only can a *bond fide* indorsee, holding it for
value, sue on it for non-payment at maturity, but
it affords an opportunity to any who may be so
disposed, to use an eminent name for the purpose
of obtaining a sum of money for a period, and

* The Athenians are said to have originated the method of discounting as at present practised,—that is, retaining the profits at
the time of the advance.

then retiring the instrument before the signature
of the acceptance could, by proper presentation,
be verified, and the forgery detected. Also subordinates in banking-houses, or any who may be
charged with the custody of bills for presentation
at maturity, should be particular in taking written
instructions respecting the non-presentment of a
bill or note; as a case may occur in which the
holder of a bill or note may know the acceptor,
and even the other parties to the instrument, to
be insolvent, and afterwards, by apparent neglect
to present at maturity, endeavour to throw the
loss on the bank. The qualifications, however,
necessary to render a man capable of presiding
over a discounting department are perhaps the
most valuable he can possess, as it is frequently
the principal source of profit to the bank. A man
must possess keen observation, a ready memory,
should have means of knowing when certain
houses are trading beyond their capital, to be
able to distinguish accommodation bills from *bonâ
fide* documents; to use all of which in discounting
operations, in a large commercial city, of necessity requires considerable experience, sound judgment, and discrimination.

18. *Indications in case of need.*

The indication ' in case of need ' will usually appear in the margin of the bill or note, and signifies that the instrument is to be taken to the house of the person or persons mentioned, who will intervene for the honour of the drawer or indorsers, as the case may be. If there be several indications ' in case of need,' application should be made to all to ascertain for whom they interfere, and the preference given to that one who will accept for honour of the prior party to the bill, calculating from the drawer.

19. *The Copy of a 'First' Bill.*

The copy of a first bill of exchange may be negotiated in the same way as a ' second ; ' the ' second ' of exchange, however, in the absence of the ' first,' is frequently accepted where the copy of a ' first ' would not be by the drawee, as it does not bear the original name of the drawer. In case of delay of the arrival of a first of exchange, a copy might be accepted for the honour of the original indorsers, as they are still liable to the holder. It is the practice abroad to furnish the copy of a bill which has not been drawn in sets.

A protest may in some cases be made on the copy
of a bill.   The person making the copy should
state distinctly ' copy,' the original with so and
so, and transcribe the whole bill with all the
indorsements, including his own.

CHAPTER VI.

BILLS OF LADING.

In one sense a bill of lading is at common law assignable, that is to say, its indorsement assigns the property, but does not transfer the contract. Now, however, by a recent statute, rights of action pass to the indorsee of a bill of lading (18 & 19 Vict. c. 111).—' Byles on Bills,' p. 2.

Bills of lading are so extensively employed in commerce, that a few words explanatory of their object may be found of service.

Upon a cargo being shipped, bills of lading— generally three, and sometimes four copies being made—are filled up with the name of the shipper; the name of the ship; her destination; the name of her captain; the particulars of the cargo, or such portion as these bills may apply to. The captain signs all the copies of the bills, retaining *one* himself, and handing over the remaining two or three to the shipper, who indorses them, either in blank or to the order of the persons to whom he has consigned the goods specified in the bills.

These bills of lading are, in other words, receipts given by the captain, in which he undertakes to deliver the goods in the same state as he received them—under certain exceptions, such as injury by ' fire, the elements, the king's enemies,' &c. The holders of the bills of lading produce one copy duly indorsed to the captain on the arrival of the ship at her destination; upon the receipt of which, he is bound to discharge the cargo to the person thus proving his title to the goods.

If goods be shipped by a vessel which has been hired by a charter-party, the master of the ship will deliver the bills of lading to the merchant who has chartered the ship; but when the ship is not chartered, but simply takes the goods generally as a carrier, then each person receives a bill of lading, which he forwards to the person who is to discharge the cargo on the arrival of the ship at its destination.

CHAPTER VII.

OF THE EXCHANGES.

THE fluctuation in the rates of exchange, or the difference in price which at various times is paid for a bill of exchange, is influenced by a great variety of circumstances, which are often unseen and unthought of by those whose daily occupation is buying and selling bills of exchange.

Our first enquiry upon entering this subject is : what gives rise to bills of exchange, independently of those bills which are now so much drawn by banks for speculation? Legitimate bills of exchange are brought into existence, in by far the greatest proportion, through the necessity which different countries are under of settling their relative indebtedness—incurred by the importation of each other's produce—independently of the precious metals. A corn merchant at New York ships a cargo to London, and instead of receiving gold or silver, or a cargo of English goods in return, draws a bill upon the consignee, and sells it upon the New York exchange. The purchaser of the bill has a payment to make in London for a cargo of English goods, and instead of sending gold or silver, or a cargo of corn, he remits the bill to his creditor, who gets it accepted, and obtains the proceeds at maturity.* It will thus be seen that at these two places, London and New York, the price of bills must depend upon the importations which have to be paid for; and the farther the importations exceed the exportations, in such proportion will the exchanges become unfavourable, until that point is reached at which it is cheaper to purchase and remit bullion. It will be seen also that the state of things must have become abnormal before the precious metals will be remitted in payment; but it stands to reason that if a merchant's expenses are very high, he must charge more on the goods he imports to the retail trader, and so on to the consumer, until the demand becomes less and the importation declines. If, however, the exportations bear a reasonable

* The purchaser here alluded to may also be drawn upon from London, and the bill used in the same way by a person who has to remit a sum of money to New York. This will depend upon agreement.

proportion to the importations, bills will be procur-
able at a moderate price, when the exchanges will
be neither severe upon buyers nor sellers of bills
of exchange.

In considering the effects of a political disturbance such as we see often happening in different
parts of the world, it will not need much reflection
to understand how great and rapid may be the disorder in commercial affairs. The recent rebellion
in the United States offers an example of what a
complete state of anarchy may be produced in a
country's commerce and currency; unlimited paper
issues causing prices to rise and gold to disappear
as a circulating medium. Next to nothing being
exported, there would be no bills to be had to pay
for imports, and the price would rise in consequence to the specie point ; gold shipments would
be liable to capture by the enemy unless in foreign
bottoms; the commercial marine would rapidly
decrease, and so forth.

Inland exchange is the employment of bills in
the discharge of debts, whereby cash remittances
are avoided, the convenience of which is obvious.
When two cities have unequal debts, the debtor
must pay the balance against it, which causes a

demand for the bills on the city to which the largest account is owing, and, as with any other article, enhances their price. London, for instance, always has a large balance in its favour, being a centre to which payments have constantly to be made, and hence the premium on bills on London. If Liverpool had to remit to London 100,000*l.* and to receive 50,000*l.* the demand for bills on London at Liverpool would exceed the supply by the difference.

Foreign exchange is in principle the same as inland, as far as the settlement of indebtedness by bills is considered, but the mode of adjustment is of necessity more complicated, when countries with different standards of value are trading with each other, their different denominations, and the depreciation which may possibly exist in the currency of one or the other.

In foreign exchanges one country always gives another a fixed sum, or piece of money, for an uncertain sum expressed by other coins. The following 'exchange list' will show some of the principal cities that receive from, or give to, London for the £ sterling. The rates given, however, are subject to constant alteration, and are increased or lessened according to the various circumstances which are ever occurring to influence the rates of exchange.

London receives from or gives to

Amsterdam	. . 12 florins	for	1*l.* sterling.
Hamburg	. . . 13 marks 9½ schill.	„	„
Paris	. . . . 25 francs 25 cents	„	„
Frankfort	. . { 120 florins 50 kreuz. to / florins 121 }	„	„
Vienna	. . . { 10 florins 40 kreuz. to / 10 florins 60 kreuz. }	„	„
Genoa	. . . }		
Milan	. . .		
Leghorn	. . . } 25 lire 25 centissimi		
Naples	. . .		
Palermo	. . /		
Madrid	. . . . 50½ pence sterling (At present worth only 46½.)	„	1 hard dollar.
Gibraltar	. . . 50 pence sterling (At present worth only 46½.)	for	„
Venice	. . . { 10 florins 40 kreuz. to / 10 florins 60 kreuz. }	for	1*l.* sterling.
St. Petersburg	. 37½ pence sterling	„	1 silver ruble.
Berlin	. . . . 6 dollars 27 silver gros.	„	1*l.* sterling.
Lisbon	. . . . 65½ pence sterling	„	1 milreis.

On account of the forced paper currency, the exchange on Vienna is, at the present moment (May 31, 1866), 13.20 to 13.30; and during the Italian war of 1859, it was as high as 16. Italy, for the reason above stated, was quoted, a month ago, as high as 30 francs (lire Italiane), but since

it has receded to 28 to 28.50.   St. Petersburg at
present is as low as 24⅜.

One is termed the 'uncertain,' the other the
'certain' price.   Paris is said to give to London
the 'uncertain' for the 'certain' price, when a
number of francs and cents are exchanged for the
£ sterling.   The quotation of the uncertain price
is termed the 'rate' or 'course of exchange.'
When there is a great demand in London for bills
on Paris, a less number of francs is given for the
£ sterling, and *vice versâ*.   If the course of exchange between London and Paris be 25 francs for
the £ sterling, and that number of francs contains
the same quantity of pure silver as 20 shillings,
then the exchange would be considered at par;
but if Paris give a higher price, the exchange
would be in favour of England and against France.
In the event of a merchant requiring to remit
money from London to Paris when the exchange
was unfavourable to England, he would adopt a
circuitous mode of payment in preference to buying a bill on Paris, which is called the 'arbitration
of exchanges;' for instance, while the bills on
Paris are at a premium in London, those on
Antwerp may be at a discount; bills also at
Antwerp may be at a discount on Paris; so if the

London merchant purchase a bill on Antwerp, directing his agent at that place to invest the proceeds in a bill on Paris, he may liquidate his debt at a cheaper rate, allowing for the additional brokerage and commissions. When three places are used in the operation it is termed '*simple arbitration*;' when more than three, '*compound arbitration.*'

What is termed the 'intrinsic par' of exchange is, the value of money between different countries, according to the accredited assay of its weight and fineness; or, in other words, the metallic worth of coins, judged according to the established value in the countries where they are current; but, except for the purpose of general information, the 'par' of exchange is not calculated—in the first place, gold being the standard of value in this country, and silver in most others; and, secondly, the gold having a fluctuating agio or premium, which would have to be taken into account, and would ultimately make it a mere valuation of bullion. The 'commercial par' is the value of money judged according to the weight and fineness, and the market prices of the metals. Two sums of money would be 'commercially' at par, when they could be exchanged for an equal quantity of the same kind of pure metal. The 'intrinsic par' of exchange may be computed from either gold or silver coins, but should be made—as a rule—from that metal in which the principal payments are made. It is, however, obvious that the par of exchange can be determined only between countries which employ the same kind of metal for the payment of their bills. The fluctuations in exchange may arise from various circumstances, political as well as commercial. A greater or less demand for money at any one place may influence its commercial value without reference to its intrinsic value; but the state of the exchanges must mainly arise from the result of the operations of exporting and importing, although it must be remembered that the mere merchandise which passes from one country to another is not the sole cause of the favourable or unfavourable state of the exchanges. A foreign loan will influence the exchanges against the country lending, and not against the borrower. It acts as an import to the lending country, and as an export to the borrowing country. The liabilities which are incurred have all an influence, whether by importing or exporting, purchasing securities, or spending money in foreign travel;

the small and the large transactions are identical in effect. It is therefore entirely erroneous to imagine that the large totals which appear as representing the imports or exports of a country are a true index of its indebtedness, or the reverse. What is termed the balance of trade may be in favour of a country as far as the actual imports and exports of merchandise are concerned; but the causes which we have enumerated above may exist to an extent entirely to counteract this. It is true the loan will have (some time or other) to be repaid, but at the time it is effected, it acts upon the exchanges by the importation of the securities of the country contracting the loan, exactly in the same way as if it were merchandise. The revenue derived from these loans, and payable at stated periods by coupons, must be taken into account, although we must not lose sight of the fact, that these permanent debts do not affect the relative indebtedness of countries, except when the time of payment arrives; neither do they affect the exchanges until the actual transfer of claims takes place. The interest due on the debts will, of necessity, be a permanent feature in the indebtedness, and must materially affect the trading capacity of a country borrowing to a large

extent, as she must either export so much more,
or import so much less.

A demand for bills of exchange arises from the
necessity of paying for importations. The supply
arises from the practice of drawing for the amount
of exportations. If the importations and exportations were to be equal, the exchange would be
nominally at par. Excess of importation causes
the exchange to advance against the importing
country, and *vice versâ*. Both importers and exporters, on all occasions, endeavour, as far as possible, to avoid the transmission of bullion, whereby
they escape the expense of freight and insurance,
and the loss of interest besides. Exporters, who
may be competing with each other, will sell their
bills below par—that is, at a discount—to avoid
bullion transmission; and, on the other side, importers, who have debts to liquidate in foreign
countries, will pay a premium for bills rather than
transmit bullion. In fact merchants, rather than
incur the necessity of sending bullion, will offer
premiums to drawers of bills, although that premium may rise, as nearly as possible, to the cost
of the bullion or specie remittance, which forcibly
proves the immense advantage of this instrument
in commercial transactions. Beyond this point—

that is, the cost of bullion or specie remittance—
the premium the importer must pay cannot rise,
and the discount the exporter must sacrifice cannot
fall. The object of an exporter is to obtain the
money for whatever he may have exported, as soon
as possible; he, therefore, draws upon the consignee or purchaser of his goods, and immediately
offers the bill for sale, if need be, at a sacrifice
rather than wait till the demand is exhausted, and
a discount established. It may so happen, however, that a bill will fetch a better price by being
drawn on a different place from that to which
the goods are shipped: for instance, a transaction
between New York and Havre, and the bill being
drawn on London. There is a variety of circumstances which may affect a bill of exchange on the
money market. First, a bill at a short date, or
sight (provided it be of first class), will command
a better *proportionate* price than one drawn at a
long date, on account of its more speedy realisation; also the contingency of failure of the parties
to the instrument at a long date is avoided. A
great consideration, too, is the state of the money
market in the country where the bill is made payable, which also affects the exchange. A bill
bought for ready money must, if it have a long

time to run, suffer a deduction in price; either the
seller or purchaser must calculate the loss of interest on a bill, according to his own money market
at home, also the time the proceeds of the bill will
take to reach him. As we have before observed,
a great demand in London for bills on Paris will
prove the exchange to be against London, and *vice
versâ*, but more especially as regards bills which
have immediately to be provided for, as the question of bullion under these circumstances may,
more or less, have to come into the calculation.
The imports and exports being somewhat balanced,
will cause the exchange to be less agitated than
if one far exceeded the other. A tight money
market will force sales, and make purchasers (unless compelled to remit) reluctant to buy. So
much less will be paid for bills drawn on a country
where the rate of interest is high; so much more
if the rate is low.* Long bills may fluctuate in
price to almost any extent, from two principal
causes existing in the country where the bills are
accepted payable. First, the fluctuation in the
value of money. Secondly, apprehensions which

---

* The rate for short bills, however, may be soon raised in a city
where there are large capitalists who are in the habit of sending
their money wherever a high rate of interest prevails.

may be felt with respect to the credit of the parties
to the bills. These will be material causes affecting the rate of exchange, and the sale of the bill.
It must be remembered that, although a certain
rate of exchange may exist to influence the price of
bills at a certain time, sellers will differ a fraction
in the price they demand, according to circumstances. The purchaser of a first-class bill must
expect to pay more, for less risk, than if he bought
a second-class bill. Even long-dated bills will
sometimes command a higher price than shorter
dates, when the credit of the parties to the long
bills stands higher in the market. It will thus be
seen that bills of exchange are subject to fluctuation from a variety of causes, and, like every other
article of commerce, will command a price according to the market value.

The term 'favourable' or 'unfavourable state
of the exchanges,' is simply this: The exchange
between London and Paris being in favour of the
former city, would indicate that the bills of London
upon Paris were at a discount, inasmuch as you
would have to give less money for a bill upon Paris
than it purported to represent; whilst the bills
drawn from Paris upon London were at a premium.
The state of the exchanges being 'unfavourable,'

proves that a great demand exists in London for
bills upon Paris, and, in consequence, renders the
necessity of exporting bullion more imminent, and
that you must give more money for a bill upon
Paris than it purported to represent. Between
Paris and London the short exchange is the most
prominent, for reasons which must suggest themselves. The exchanges being effected in this
way (viz. the difference between the payments
which have to be made between one country and
another) is not the only cause to which the
fluctuations can be traced. The currencies of two
countries (between which bills of exchange may
be operating) being dissimilar will affect the exchange if one of them be at a premium. Political
causes will frequently frighten sellers to part with
their bills at a great sacrifice in order to insure
immediate payment; and such a thing has been
heard of as a panic in the money market when the
exchange has been favourable.* A profit on the
shipment of specie is only obtained under exceptional circumstances, such as a great distance and
difficulty of communication existing between two

* Foreign exchanges will fall if the market price of bullion rise
above the mint price; also an alteration in the mint price will affect
the par of exchange with other countries.

commercial places, and where the want of sellers
of bills to receive the equivalent in specie was
anticipated, whereby the bills might be bought up
below the specie point. Another cause for the
fluctuation of exchange will be the transfer of a
large amount of capital from one country to another, where a high rate of interest is to be obtained.
An advance in the Bank of England rate of discount is invariably followed by a turn of the
exchanges in favour of England; and a fall in
the rate immediately produces an opposite effect.
The reason of this is easily to be accounted for.
The high rate of interest ruling in London would
cause a demand for bills on that city, with
a view of using the proceeds of those bills in
obtaining that high rate of interest. Speculative
purchasers of bills are sure to ascertain the difference of rate in the country where the bill is
drawn and the country where it is made payable,
as this may enable them to obtain more for a bill
on a country where the rate either has risen or is
likely to rise. Hence we see the great importance
which is attached to the changes of the rate of
discount. There are many Continental cities which
hold large amounts in bills on London, and, if the
rate of interest here falls below the Continental

rate, those bills will be immediately sent to England, and the gold returned to be invested in the higher rate of interest ruling on the Continent. A rise in the price of bills *on* England is sure to be accompanied by a fall in the price of foreign bills in England. We find that the fluctuations in exchange also arise from a depreciation of one or both currencies, or the transfer of any quantity of bullion or specie from one country to another, either of which will produce an effect in proportion to the magnitude of the cause. We will endeavour to give two examples illustrative of these two causes of fluctuation. First, a depreciation of the currency is due to the rise of the market price of gold above the mint price, allowing a margin for the metal being changed from one form to another, and the foreign exchange falling lower than the limit of the real exchange; thus: the *nominal* exchange between London and Amsterdam fell more than 20 per cent. against England in 1694, on account of the depreciation of her currency, at the same time the *real* exchange was in her favour. Secondly, to illustrate the fluctuation of exchange as caused by transmission of bullion, suppose England is driven to the American market for corn, on account of the failure of the harvest, and that a large quantity of corn is shipped to England without America having made equal purchases from England, the balance of trade must be against England, to meet which bullion must be remitted; bills on New York will immediately be at a premium; the exchange will be adverse to England; and, if the premium on bills rises beyond a certain point, an efflux of bullion must be the inevitable result. These are the two prime causes of the fluctuation in exchange; and the fundamental principle upon which the price of bills rests is the ' *balance of indebtedness.* '

CHAPTER VIII.

OF CURRENCY.

A CHAPTER on currency cannot, perhaps, be better opened than by quoting two paragraphs from the writings of the patriarch of political economy, Adam Smith. In chapter iv. of 'The Wealth of Nations,' upon the subject 'Of the Origin and Use of Money,' he begins thus:

'When the division of labour has been once thoroughly established, it is but a very small part of a man's wants which the produce of his own labour can supply. He supplies the far greater part of them by exchanging that surplus part of the produce of his own labour, which is over and above his own consumption, for such parts of the produce of other men's labour as he has occasion for. Every man thus lives by exchanging, or becomes, in some measure, a merchant; and the society itself grows to be what is properly a commercial society.

'But, when the division of labour first begun to take place, this power of exchanging must frequently have been very much clogged and embarrassed in its operations. One man, we shall suppose, has more of a certain commodity than he himself has occasion for, while another has less. The former, consequently, would be glad to dispose of, and the latter to purchase, a part of this superfluity. But, if this latter should chance to have nothing that the former stands in need of, no exchange can be made between them. The butcher has more meat in his shop than he himself can consume, and the brewer and the baker would each of them be willing to purchase a part of it; but they have nothing to offer in exchange except the different productions of their respective trades, and the butcher is already provided with all the bread and beer which he has immediate occasion for. No exchange can in this case be made between them. He cannot be their merchant, nor they his customers; and they are all of them thus mutually less serviceable to one another. In order to avoid the inconvenience of such situations, every prudent man, in every period of society after the first establishment of the division of labour, must naturally have endeavoured to manage his

affairs in such a manner as to have at all times
by him, besides the peculiar produce of his own
industry, a certain quantity of some one commodity or other, such as he imagined few people
would be likely to refuse in exchange for the produce of their industry.' The great advantage of
coined money for currency purposes, we are told,
first presented itself to the Lydians ; as coined
money, however, will be treated separately in the
chapter upon coins, we shall simply confine our
attention to the investigation of the question of
currency generally, as a commodity employed for
the measurement of the value in exchange of all
other articles.

Mr. John Stuart Mill, in his 'Principles of Political Economy,' vol. ii., p. 168, says: 'The introduction of money is a mere addition of one
more commodity, of which the value is regulated
by the same laws as that of all other commodities ;
and that money has little to do except to furnish
a convenient mode of comparing values.' And
again, at page 172: ' In international, as in ordinary
domestic interchanges, money is to commerce what
oil is to machinery, or railways to locomotion, a
contrivance to diminish friction.'

Gold and silver have been long accepted as the

most fitted for a metallic currency, as combining
the greatest worth with the least fluctuation in
value, in the most convenient form. Gold being a
more expensive metal by about fifteen times than
silver, will be naturally employed only by rich
countries as their standard of value, and silver by
poorer countries. The value in exchange of gold
and silver, like all other commodities, will depend
upon the labour required for their production.
The currency of countries can never become super-
abundant, for increasing the quantity will of necessity diminish the value. A continued increase
in the metallic currency of a country raises prices,
which attracts commodities from other countries,
in return for which the money flows out until the
normal level is again reached. Mr. Ricardo says:
' Gold and silver having been chosen for the general
medium of circulation, they are by the competition of commerce distributed in such proportions
amongst the different countries of the world as to
accommodate themselves to the natural traffic
which would take place if no such metals existed,
and the trade between countries were purely a
trade of barter.' The great difference which is
known to exist between the metallic currency of
England and France will demonstrate how much

M

more costly the French system must be as compared with the English, with whom many more
times the amount of mutual indebtedness is settled
simply with the aid of paper. Whether the extent
to which the metallic basis has been diminished in
England causes more loss to the community generally by the more rapid fluctuations in the price
which must be paid for it or not, is a matter for
closer investigation ; but there can be little doubt
that the damage which may be caused by too small
a metallic basis, when commerce is temporarily
deranged by natural or unnatural agencies, can
bring far more permanent loss upon a nation than
the most expensive circulating medium that can
be devised. The fact can never be got rid of, that,
however small it may be desirable that the metallic
pivot should be upon which the paper medium
revolves, and however large the profit may be from
such economy, every pound upon paper that represents twenty shillings must if required throw off
its disguise ; and if the occasion suddenly presents
itself when the paper obligations of a nation unex-
pectedly and on a very large scale are required to
be converted into gold, then happens the crisis
which is the inevitable consequence of a demand
to fulfil engagements which would never have been

contracted had such a contingency even been conceived possible; and it is the fatal mistake which
so many engaged in mercantile affairs make, of
spreading their operations over too wide an area
in proportion to their real capital, that causes so
much disaster, when the assistance of discounting,
&c., to which they have become so accustomed, is
suddenly curtailed, and perhaps cut off altogether.
When all works smoothly, and the great products
of the earth yield a fair average of what is expected
of them, then those engaged in their importation
and exportation are maintained by their distribu-
tion to the masses; but failure in the yield of
any of the great products of the earth carries loss
and ruin to the doors of thousands: a famine caused
by a bad harvest produces the same effect among
those who subsist upon bread as a famine among
merchants and traders when the credit they have
been long accustomed to is suddenly withdrawn.
Conceive a large manufacturer who sells his goods
to wholesale dealers on six months' credit, and has
been in the habit of discounting their acceptances
and making fresh goods with the proceeds, his capital in the greatest part being the machinery and premises where the manufacturing goes on; his banker
raising the rate of interest, so that a large part of his

profit is eaten up, is already bad enough ; but when,
from a general panic, the banker's available funds
are required to meet current demands, what becomes
of the manufacturer when the assistance which has
become so indispensable is withdrawn altogether?
He has also purchased the raw material, and in
his turn has accepted bills which will now perhaps
become useless in the hands of the creditor. So
distrust spreads itself, and all the currency laws
that can ever be devised will never make capital so
elastic, or money—which is its representative—
available for sudden emergencies, any more than
supplies of corn can be created when God does not
think fit to give the increase.

A currency is undoubtedly in the most desirable
form, and is most perfect, when consisting entirely
of paper, *when* that paper can at all times be exchanged for the gold or silver which it purports to
represent. Gold and silver are the dearest form of
currency, paper is the cheapest.

When gold was first used as part of the currency,
Dr. Adam Smith informs us ' it was not considered
as a legal tender for a long time after it was coined
into money. The proportion between the values
of gold and silver money was not fixed by any
public law or proclamation, but was left to be

settled by the market. If a debtor offered payment
in gold, the creditor might either reject such payment altogether, or accept it at such a valuation
of the gold as he and his debtor could agree upon.'
In this way it will be seen that all persons would
discharge their debts in one or the other of these
metals which was most favourable to the discharge
of their debts at the time. The double standard
in France encourages this system in the present
day, and can be the means of causing the dearer
metal to disappear from circulation for a time, as
it would no longer be the standard, and be worth
more when melted into bullion than remaining in
the shape of coins. The great inconvenience of a
constantly-fluctuating standard was ably shown by
Mr. Locke, and other writers who followed him;
but not till the year 1816 could the great importance of fixing the standard be sufficiently impressed
upon the minds of those through whose agency
alone such a reform could be legally effected.

If the silver currency were coined to an unlimited
extent, it would sink in value as compared with gold,
and therefore the Government have taken upon
themselves to stop the coinage of silver when they
may deem such a course expedient; in addition to
which it is a legal tender only to the extent of 40s.

Some persons are under the impression that a
country which has a large metallic currency is very
rich. On the contrary, it is a waste of resources
instead of an indication of wealth. The object of
all nations now is to economise their currency as
much as possible. To achieve this end, the great
thing to do is to establish banks everywhere, which
will drive the currency rapidly into all channels
where it is required to stimulate industry. Every
man in a country may walk about with his pockets
full of gold; but this will not help to cultivate the
ground, to work mines, or to grow coffee, cotton,
tea, or assist in bringing forward any produce of
the earth. There is much waste in this respect in
countries which are thinly populated, where the
difficulties of getting from one town to another are
great. When people cannot obtain their money
without much trouble and delay, they are unwilling
to deposit in a bank even when they are paid interest for its use. It can easily be imagined what
the loss would be of erecting a costly steam-engine,
and then, instead of applying it to the various uses
of grinding corn or making paper, it were allowed
to remain motionless. If a number of people walk
about with their pockets full of sovereigns for long
periods together, a precisely similar loss is taking

place the whole time. Each sovereign has so much value in exchange, in the same way as a part of the steam-engine, in proportion to the amount of labour necessary to its production; and either causes a loss to the community by not doing the work for which it was created. At a certain period of Spanish history her soldiers are said to have been provided with gold swords but no shirts; and this will serve as an instance to prove of how little proportionate value gold becomes when it ceases to be employed as a medium for procuring other commodities.

The absolute necessity of banks in thoroughly utilising the currency is established by showing how the money of one man, instead of lying idle in his coffers, and representing so much latent power, may be lent to another, and by him to a third, for the furtherance of their respective schemes, and will pass again into a bank to be busily employed in a hundred other transactions. In this respect, paper is considered the most perfect form of currency, although some authorities go so far as to consider that paper debases the currency. It must, however, be obvious that as long as the paper either continues to command the amount of legal metallic currency for which it was first

accepted by the public, or to purchase bullion at the
mint price, it cannot debase the currency. Paper
currency has a considerable advantage over metallic,
inasmuch as it cannot depreciate by abrasion. A
large paper currency is unmistakable proof of a
country's prosperity, *while* that paper continues to
be equivalent to its nominal value in gold. The
great problem which the legislature has to solve
for the benefit of the currency and banking is to
devise such a system as will prevent paper from
being issued in such excessive quantities as to lower
the standard of value altogether, and consequently
raise the market price of gold. The issue of as-
signats during the French Revolution, April 1790,
produced the most disastrous effects, as much as
350 millions sterling being in circulation in France
and its dependencies. But, on the other hand, as
Adam Smith truly remarks, 'the substitution of
paper for gold money replaces a very expensive
instrument of commerce with one much less costly,
and sometimes equally convenient—a new wheel
comes into operation which is both cheaper to erect
and to maintain in efficiency.' It appears, then,
that the great object is, so to regulate the issue of
paper that banks shall preserve the equilibrium of
the currency by withdrawing the excess and sup-

plying the deficiency. A fixed circulation of paper can only remain so while the population and industry remain comparatively stationary ; but as a city increases in size and commercial importance, so must the machinery for its pecuniary transactions be enlarged.

We find that all countries have been engaged in discovering the most portable and valuable of the metals to adopt as a currency, in which would be represented the greatest power of commanding services or things, and of the most convenient form for carrying about the person; and it must be apparent to the meanest understanding that other than an entirely metallic currency *must* come into operation as civilisation advances. Immense transactions take place involving large payments, and, as a natural consequence, paper representing the amount must come into use to obviate the trouble and labour of transferring a large amount of coin. Agricultural countries progress slower in the accumulation of wealth, on account of the circulation of their currencies being more languid. Poland may be cited as a country engaged principally in agriculture, and consequently very poor. England and Holland, on the contrary, have a very small proportion of their populations engaged in agriculture, and both are rich countries. The Spaniards entirely overlooked the great axiom that money was only wealth when employed in setting industry in motion, and worse than useless when amassed in large quantities, as they did after their American conquests, whereby other countries gained by the sale of their manufactures to Spain, while her internal trade languished, until protection was obliged to be called in; and eventually smuggling ensued to such an extent that, while the cotton goods of England were prohibited from being brought into the country, the officers of the Government were selling them at Madrid 30 per cent. beyond their Manchester value.

The most celebrated Act that has been passed for the rectification of the disorders which had on so many occasions paralysed our money market previous to the year 1844, was passed into law through the instrumentality of Sir Robert Peel at the renewal of the Bank of England charter, which was granted in 1844. On two occasions has the action of this law been suspended by Government, the first of which took place about three years after the measure was enacted. As an additional proof of how far this measure has fallen short of what was expected of it, we may quote a question

which was put by a member of the House of Commons to the governor of the Bank of England in
1848: ' You have described, as part of the operation of the Act of 1844, that you were during the
year 1847 obliged to lend consols instead of notes, on account of the limit prescribed by the Act
—that you borrowed consols in April—that you were obliged to raise the rate of interest to 9 per
cent.—that you refused loans on Exchequer bills —that there was a pressure in April and a panic
in October—and that Government were obliged to interpose by a letter, in order to protect the public
from the restrictive effects of the Act.* Do you call that a satisfactory history of any system?'†
The observation may be made that the state of commerce altogether, just previous to 1848, was
such that no single institution, under the circumstances in which the Bank was then placed, could
bear up against such an exceptional and abnormal state of things. Commercial affairs, doubtless,
can be so paralysed that no bank, as they are at present constituted, can withstand the strain. It

* It was found necessary again to suspend this celebrated Act in
May 1866, when advances were made by the Bank of England to
the unprecedented extent of 4,000,000l. in one day. See Appendix.
† J. W. Gilbart, 'Treatise on Banking,' vol. i. p. 150.

is quite impossible to predict to what extent the crises of 1847 and 1857 may be re-enacted; but it is certain that, unless the provisions of the Act of 1844 are reconsidered, and the weakness which both departments of the Bank suffer from by their separation is strengthened by exterior co-operation, we shall never see the national currency doing its work—during periods when money is difficult to obtain—without rapid and unnatural fluctuations.

There is a prevalent and erroneous idea in the minds of many people that banks have the power to force into circulation as much paper money as they like, and that by such means, at the will of paper issuers, the currency may be expanded *ad infinitum* so long as any profit is to be reaped by such expansion. If too much—that is to say, more than can be consumed—of any other commodity is produced, its value becomes reduced until the surplus has disappeared, when the ordinary price is again reached. As *metallic* money is affected by all the peculiarities which affect other commodities, and has its price determined by the amount of labour necessary for its production, when supplied in quantities beyond the capacity of the period to utilise or consume it,

it falls in exchangeable value, or, which is equivalent, causes the prices of other things to rise,
other things having previously been measured by
its value. So long, therefore, as *paper* money is
accepted by the public as equal in exchangeable
value to the gold it represents, the currency is
increased in the same degree as if so much more
gold is in circulation. Instead of the gold falling
in exchangeable value, as it would do, its representative, the paper, is returned upon the issuers
until that amount of currency has been reached
which is sufficient to enable the population to
transfer their goods according to the demand and
supply of such goods at the time; and the amount
of the currency can only be influenced, either side
of such natural point, by the fluctuations of price
and production, and by an absence or otherwise of
that knowledge which in the present day enables
the foremost countries so greatly to economise
their currencies, and especially the metallic portion, by the aid of banking institutions.

In 1832 Mr. Tooke reported to a committee of
the House of Commons—when the question of the
Bank charter was being discussed—that, ' as far
as my researches have gone, in every signal instance of a rise or fall of prices, the rise or fall has

preceded, and therefore could not be the effect of,
an enlargement or contraction of the Bank circulation.'*

A rise of prices generally has the effect of causing people to spend more, under the belief that
the increased charge will be only temporary and
they need not deny themselves. If bread and
meat rise 2d. or 3d. a pound, or even less, in a
large city, it will stand to reason that the payments made by all purchasers of these articles of
food will be increased by such proportion; and, if
the·majority of them draw their weekly cheque
upon their bankers for so much more than usual,
the rise of prices will be followed by an expansion
in the circulation of bank notes. When such
prices recede, or fall below the ordinary prices,
the circulation of bank notes will be contracted, à
priori, in a similar manner.

There is, however, a vast number of causes
which influence the fluctuations of the currency,
and which at some periods cause very great competition for money, or credit, which is the same
thing; the result of which is a rise in the rate of

---

* This has reference to a temporary rise of prices from a scarcity
of certain commodities, and is quite distinct from a permanent increase in that commodity which is used for the circulating medium.

discount. The immense competition at present in the city of London appears to promise no return to 2 or 3 per cent. for loans, &c., as we have seen. Every shilling that can be laid hold of is eagerly seized by this or that finance company or bank, who bid against each other to obtain deposits. In this way enormous sums of money are collected by these institutions at short call, and are employed in a hundred enterprises where a larger rate of interest can be obtained for the loan than is paid to the depositors. This works all very well until the depositors become panic stricken, and all demand their money at once. The stages necessary for procuring the money which is lent to a railway company, for instance, for nine or twelve months, need not be gone through; suffice it to show that a healthy rise in the rate of discount, occasioned by an increase in the legitimate trade of the country, becomes unduly augmented by the pressure of these companies for similar accommodation, when even a part of their deposits are withdrawn from distrust or otherwise. There is also a class of capitalless speculators, who are often encouraged in their bottomless enterprises by obtaining credits with certain companies, which is an easier method than getting cash in the ordinary way of discount.

It will be obvious that, when possible, many of these bills will be discounted, and will be the very paper to do the most mischief when the abnormal pressure comes, being, as a rule, based upon nothing. Many of these companies, in order to obtain any business at all, have encouraged the creation of a great deal of bad paper, and thus a dangerous and permanently increased demand for credit and accommodation has become established, which must tend to enhance its price and, consequently, keep up the rate of discount.

CHAPTER IX.

ON BANK-NOTES.

Historical Memoir from the Establishment of the Bank of England — Suspension of Cash Payments, 1793 — Resumption of Cash Payments, 1821 — Panic of the Year 1825 — Renewal of the Bank Charter, 1833 — Bank Acts of 1844 and 1845 — Clauses of the Act of 1844 relating to Bank of England Notes — Clauses of the Act of 1844 relating to Country Bank Notes — Effects of the Act on the Country Note Issues — Irish and Scotch Bank Acts — Present State of the Fixed Issues — Remarks on the Regulation of Bank Note Issues.

THE only approach to paper money in this country, previous to the establishment of the Bank of England, was the issue of receipts by the goldsmiths for money lodged in their hands, which receipts were frequently circulated in the same way that bank-notes are at present.

Correctly speaking, the issue of bank-notes commenced with the Bank of England, in 1694, although there was at that time a most important difference between those documents and the issues in use now, inasmuch as the Bank then allowed interest at the rate of 2d. per cent. per diem on its

notes. By the charter of the Bank, it was prohibited from borrowing in excess of its capital,
which was at first fixed at 1,200,000*l.*; and it would
seem that the full amount was issued very quickly,
for, in a pamphlet published by Mr. Godfrey, the
deputy-governor in 1695, he mentions that the
interest paid on notes was 36,000*l.*, which would
be about the sum required if the limit was attained;
the practice of allowing interest on notes seems,
however, to have been very soon discontinued.

Bank-notes, shortly after their introduction, had
a very serious ordeal to go through, and one which
cannot be attributed in justice to the authorities of
the Bank. For some years previous to the establishment of the Bank of England, the scandalous
custom of clipping the silver coin had been carried
on to a great extent, in spite of severe laws enacted
against it. In the summer of 1695 the evil had
gone to such a length, that thirty shillings in silver
coin was required to purchase a guinea. In the
early part of 1696 a new silver coinage was issued
to the Bank. Previously, silver had almost disappeared from circulation, it having been exported
to purchase gold, the profit thereon being so great.
When the new silver was coined, there naturally
ensued a rush to procure it, and the Bank was

obliged to repay, in silver of full weight, the notes
it had previously issued in exchange for clipped
and debased coin. The loss thereon was of course
very large; but that was not the whole of the evil,
the new silver could not be procured quickly
enough to meet the demand, and in consequence
a notification was published partially suspending
cash payments.

Bank-notes on this fell to 20 per cent. discount,
and to counteract this an expedient was adopted
of a very bold, but, as it turned out, entirely suc-
cessful, nature. This was an increase of capital,
the subscriptions to which were to be received *at
par*, in bank-notes, which stood then at the above-
mentioned discount, and in exchequer tallies which
were still more depreciated. Upwards of 1,000,000*l.*
was thus subscribed, and the withdrawal of that
sum from circulation had the effect of raising the
remaining part to its nominal value. It should
here be mentioned that, although Parliament did
in the year 1697 pledge themselves not to establish
by legislative enactment any corporation in opposition to the Bank of England, there was nothing to
prevent any private body of men from doing so
until the year 1707, when a bill was passed prohibiting any number of persons exceeding six from

issuing notes on demand, or for any less tenor than
six months; and as the idea was then prevalent
that banking could not be profitably carried on
without the privilege of issuing notes, this prohibition effectually prevented any opposition to the
Bank of England by the establishment of other
banks on the joint-stock principle. Parliament,
though thus careful of the interests of the Bank
of England, failed to take any precaution to stop
the issue of notes to an unlimited extent by country
private bankers, the consequence of which was
that shopkeepers turned bankers in all directions,
and flooded the country with their worthless paper.
A strange anomaly this, to prohibit a corporation
of known wealth and respectability from issuing
notes, and allow individuals, in some cases not
worth sixpence, to do so to an extent only limited
by the faith of their customers.

This monopoly was in full force over the whole
of England until 1826, when it was partially done
away with by restricting its operation to a radius
of sixty-five miles from London; and in 1833, as
regards deposits, the whole country was exempted
from the sway of the Bank of England.

In 1759 notes were first issued for 15*l.* and 10*l.*,
the minimum having previously been 20*l.*; no

further alteration took place until 1795, when 5*l.* notes were used.

It is worthy of remark that about 1781, the use of cheques becoming more general, the London private bankers discontinued the issue of notes;* and from that time have never renewed it, although not prevented by legislative enactment until 1844.

We have now to consider an episode in the history of the nation which, to a commercial people like ourselves, must always be looked back upon with shame and regret; we allude to the suspension of cash payments. Various causes have been assigned for this unfortunate step, the management of the Bank being very roughly censured by some writers. Sinclair, in his 'History of the Revenue,' † quotes the opinion of a contemporary, and especially mentions that he agrees with it, to the effect 'that the conduct pursued by the Bank of England, for a considerable time previous to the suspension of the payment of its notes, almost warrants the suspicion that instead of really dreading that suspension as an evil, they

* Macleod, vol. ii. p. 63.
† Sinclair's 'Hist. of Revenue,' vol. ii. p. 307.

rather looked to it as an advantage.' There is
no doubt that the holders of bank stock did
benefit largely by the suspension, as the following
figures will testify.

In the year 1797, when the restriction commenced, the highest price of bank stock was 146,
the lowest 115; * we will take the price every five
years down to the final resumption in 1821 :—

Years	Highest	Lowest
1802 . . .	207 . . .	178
1807 . . .	235 . . .	208
1812 . . .	232 . . .	212
1817 . . .	294 . . .	220
1821 . . .	240 . . .	221

For several years prior to 1797 the dividend on
bank stock had been at the rate of 7 per cent. per
annum. In 1807 it was raised to 10 per cent., in
addition to which from 1797 to 1816 the pro-
prietors had bonuses on their capital presented
to them of the following amounts, viz. :—

17½ per cent. in Navy Five per Cents.
15   „   in Money.
25   „   in Bank Stock.†

These advantages truly were very great; but
before condemning the directors for acting as they

* Francis' 'Hist. of Bank,' vol. ii. p. 261.
† Ibid. p. 276.

did, the difficulties of their position should be
well considered, and the probable effects of a
different system to that adopted duly weighed.
A clause in the Act of 1694 prohibited the Bank
from advancing money to the Government under
the penalty of a fine of treble the amount so advanced. In 1793 Mr. Pitt introduced and quickly
passed an Act repealing this clause,* which practically took the management of the Bank out of
the hands of the directors, unless they resorted
to the extreme measure of refusing to pay the
drafts of the Government, and thereby proclaim-
ing a national bankruptcy. In his extreme need
of money Mr. Pitt did not fail to make use of this
resource, and to such an extent that by an account
dated February 10, 1797, we find the advances
amounted to 7,185,645l., exclusive of 400,000l. for
arrears of interest.† It must be understood that
this is altogether distinct from the permanent
debt due to the Bank of 11,686,800l., which was
included in the national debt accounts as funded
debt, and was the subscribed capital of the Bank;
the advances in question formed part of the un-
funded debt.

* Sinclair's ' Hist. of Revenue,' vol. iii. p. 26.
† Francis' ' Hist. of Bank,' vol. i. p. 229.

The enormous subsidies this country was sending abroad to aid its allies on the continent in the
struggle against Napoleon, had caused an immense drain on the metallic reserves of the Bank
for the last year or two; while the diminution of
the provincial bankers' issues since 1793 (estimated by Mr. Thornton at one half) rendered an
extra supply of bullion necessary to supply the
deficiency which also was drawn from the Bank,
and altogether had reduced the stock of specie so
low that the directors in their anxiety to provide
for their own safety used every means to get
notes in, and to such purpose that in five weeks
prior to February 25, 1797, the circulation was
reduced from 10,550,830*l.* to 8,640,250*l.** The
contraction of the note circulation increased the
requirement for gold; the probability of invasion
induced hoarding, and a run on, and consequent
stoppage of, two large banks at Newcastle on
February 20 caused a complete panic, which
lasted all through the week, by which time the
bullion at the Bank was brought down to
1,272,000*l.* On Sunday, February 26, 1797, a
cabinet council was held, when the resolution was

* 'Lords' Report, 1797,' p. 177.

arrived at to suspend cash payments, and instructions to that effect were given both to the Bank of England and the Bank of Ireland. From that date to May 1, 1821, this country had what it is to be hoped it will never see again—an inconvertible paper currency.

It appears that at the time of the suspension the assets of the Bank exceeded its liabilities by 3,826,890l. exclusive of the permanent debt of the Government.

Committees of both houses were immediately appointed to investigate the affairs of the Bank, and the causes and advisability of the suspension. The directors attributed it to the advances to Government; merchants to the sudden contraction of the note circulation.

Mr. Macleod,* after some remarks in which he agrees with the merchants, says: 'From the foregoing consideration, as well as the weight of authority on the subject, we can scarcely have any room to doubt that the suspension of cash payments was brought about at that particular time by the erroneous policy of the directors. We must in candour state that it appears open

* Macleod, 'On Banking,' vol. ii. p. 98.

to much doubt whether any management, however skilful, could ultimately have saved them from such a disaster during some period of the war.' But he also says: ' As the suspension, then, must, we think, have taken place sooner or later, it was probably advantageous for the country that it did occur so early in the struggle.' * Although, as already mentioned, the resumption of cash payments did not take place until the year 1821, when the order for suspension was issued, the 24th of June in the same year was the date given for resuming, but after one or two extensions of the time, a month after the conclusion of a definitive treaty of peace was finally fixed as the limit.

An Act was passed in 1797 to remedy the want of small change by allowing small notes to be issued; in England below 5*l.*, in Scotland below 1*l.*

The following figures, extracted from ' Francis' History of the Bank of England,' will show the wonderful effect the suspension and the issue of small notes had upon the Bank circulation; unfortunately the country banks at that time made

* Macleod, ' On Banking,' vol. ii. p. 100.

no returns, so that it can only be a matter of estimate as to what extent they were influenced.

		Circulation.		Bullion.
Feb. 28, 1792	.	11,307,000	. .	6,468,000
„ 1797	.	9,675,000	. .	1,086,000
„ 1802	.	15,187,000	. :	4,153,000
„ 1807	.	16,951,000	. .	6,143,000
„ 1812	.	23,408,000	. .	2,983,000
„ 1817	.	27,398,000	. .	9,681,000
„ 1821	.	23,885,000	. .	11,870,000
„ 1823	.	18,392,000	. .	10,384,000*

By this it will be seen that while the circulation, i.e. the profitable part of the Bank business, rapidly expanded, the bullion, or unprofitable part of its resources, was usually lower than before the inconvertible system began. Although it is not possible to tell the amount of the increase of the country bank-notes, there cannot be the slightest doubt that, taking into consideration the number of new banks started during the period, it must have been many millions.

In 1797 the number of country banks was 270; in 1810, 721—a threefold increase in the space of 13 years. In 1813 they had risen to 940.

It will be scarcely worth while to follow the course of the paper currency through its vicissitudes for the next few years, or to trace the

* Francis' 'Hist. of Bank,' vol. ii. p. 277.

gradual depreciation, first of Bank of Ireland, and later of Bank of England notes, a depreciation which the Bank directors in both countries earnestly denied, contending that gold had risen instead of the note having fallen in value. It is as well to pass over this, and like controversies of that day, as matters on which there is now no difference of opinion. Mr. Macleod gives a table showing the market price of bullion,* and consequent *real* value of the bank-note at various times during the restriction, by which it appears that down to 1804 the depreciation was but nominal, after that time it became gradually worse; on August 6, 1813, the price of bullion was 5*l.* 10*s.*, making the 1*l.* note equivalent to 14*s.* 2*d.* in coin; this was the extreme point of depreciation.

The Peace of Amiens, concluded March 27, 1802, compelled the Bank to be ready to pay bullion in a month from that date, but Mr. Addington relieved it of the necessity by persuading parliament to prolong the restriction until March 1, 1803; it was then put off to the following session, by which time war had again broken out, so the resumption of cash payments was deferred until

* Macleod's 'History of Banking,' vol. ii. p. 221.

six months after the conclusion of a treaty of peace. This period expired in March 1815, but again was the evil day postponed to July 1816, afterwards to 1818, and finally, by the provision of Peel's Currency Bill, a gradual resumption took place.

This celebrated Bill enacted that between February 1 and October 1, 1820, the Bank should cash its notes in bullion at 4*l*. 1*s*. per ounce; from October 1, 1820, to May 1, 1821, at 3*l*. 19*s*. 6*d*.; and from the last date to May 1, 1823, at 3*l*. 17*s*. 10½*d*.; in each case the notes presented were to represent the value of 60 ounces. On May 1, 1823, the restriction acts were to expire finally. In 1821 a Bill was passed to allow the Bank to resume its payments in cash, May 1, 1821, which it accordingly did on that date. The Act of 1819 had provided that the issue of country notes for 1*l*. and 2*l*. should be stopped in two years from the Bank of England resuming cash payments; but it was found in 1822 that the rapid contraction of the currency owing to the enactment of Peel's Bill, had caused such a diminution in prices generally that it was deemed wise to respite the small notes till 1833.

This had a most injurious effect—the country

banks poured forth their paper in all directions, prices rose rapidly, and speculation was engendered to a vast extent; bubble companies started up by dozens, and loans were contracted with the greatest ease by foreign powers; all went well and prosperously till the latter end of 1825, when the bullion in the Bank began to diminish, and the directors in consequence contracted the discount accommodation to the public. Then the companies formed by the speculation of the hour found their shares fast falling in price, the country banks were beset for cash in exchange for notes, the whole ending in the panic of 1825. It is said that the discovery of a number of 1*l*. notes at the Bank of England ready for circulation, and the issue thereof with the consent of the Government, was of the most important service in restoring confidence in the country districts. The panic was, however, the death-blow to the small notes, as after February 1826 no more stamps were issued, and in April 1829 small notes were finally abolished in this country. Government at this time intended also to extinguish the Scotch and Irish 1*l*. and 2*l*. notes, but the opposition to it, especially in Scotland, where it was assisted by the powerful pen of Sir Walter Scott, was too strong for ministers to meddle with, and the small notes exist to this day in both the sister countries.

The panic of 1825 led to two other important measures, both with the same end in view—the improvement of the country circulation—viz. the establishment of branches of the Bank of England in the larger towns, and the partial abolition of the Bank monopoly by the permission to open joint-stock banks of issue beyond sixty-five miles from London. We may remark *en passant* that in the debates relative to these changes, both Mr. Huskisson and Sir Robert Peel advocated the limited liability system for banking companies, which has lately been so largely developed.

The important step of making notes of the Bank of England a legal tender was taken at the renewal of the charter in 1833, when it was declared that the tender of notes for any sum above 5l. was legal in England and Wales, except by the Bank of England itself. This measure was strongly debated at the time, and among its opponents was Sir Robert Peel, but it was carried on a division by 214 to 156.

In this Act was inserted a clause to the effect that the exclusive privileges of the Bank of England did not extend to the prohibition of joint-stock banks within sixty-five miles of London, provided they were not banks of issue.

This clause was strongly protested against by the Bank, on the ground that the negotiations with the ministry previous to the renewal were carried on with the understanding that the privileges of the Bank were to be preserved intact. This was strictly true. At the time these communications passed there can be no doubt that both parties were of opinion that the phraseology of the charter prevented the establishment of banks, either of issue or deposit, within sixty-five miles of London; but when the law officers had been consulted and gave their opinion adversely to the Bank, Lord Althorp determined to avail himself of it, and answered the directors by saying that the stipulation was that their privileges should not be lessened, to which he would strictly adhere, but that he could not consent to improve their position by any new enactment. Now, whatever may be the general opinion respecting the policy of curtailing the exclusive rights of the Bank as regards the public, it will doubtless be conceded that it was rather sharp practice towards the corporation. The directors did not feel strong enough to resist the Government, so they did the best thing possible under the circumstances, submitted with a good grace.

The charter was renewed in 1833 for twenty-one years from August 1, 1834, but power was reserved by the Government to suspend it after the expiration of ten years if a twelvemonths' notice was given of the intention.

Within the next few years there were two serious disturbances in the money market, but arising from very different causes; the first culminating in the latter end of the year 1836, the second in 1839. The harvests of 1832-3-4 were very abundant, and the price of corn in consequence fell extremely low, which although a severe trial for the agricultural, was a source of great prosperity to the manufacturing interest. Railway schemes were starting, and speculation of all kinds increasing, the new joint-stock banks giving great facilities by credit and discounts; which latter were immediately re-discounted, until the Bank of England issued a notice to the effect that all bills bearing the indorsement of a joint-stock bank would be refused discount, whatever other indorsements they might have. America was about this time re-establishing a metallic currency, and drawing large sums

o

from this country in exchange for securities. Two
large joint-stock banks failed—the 'Northern and
Central' in England, the 'Agricultural and Commercial' in Ireland—during the month of November 1836, and of course created a great deal of
uneasiness, but the Bank of England by giving
large accommodation seems to have averted the
storm.

The second disturbance was owing to very
different causes : following the plentiful harvests
above mentioned was a succession of bad ones,
causing an enormous demand for corn from
abroad, which in due course necessitated an export of bullion to pay for it. The Bank of England was obliged to resort to an artificial means
of getting the gold back, and the expedient
adopted was this : by arrangement, Messrs. Baring
drew for about two millions sterling on Paris
bankers, the Bank of France engaging to pay the
drafts even should the acceptors not be in a position to take them up at maturity. This had the
effect of stopping the drain ; but so low had the
cash fallen that, on September 2, 1839, the total
amount at the Bank was 2,406,000l.,* and it is

* Macleod's 'Hist. of Banking,' vol. ii. p. 255.

said that but for this relief it would have been necessary to suspend payment.

Having rapidly glanced at the history, so to speak, of the paper currency, we come to the consideration of the Act of 1844, which is now the regulator of the note circulation of the United Kingdom; for although the parts affecting Scotland and Ireland formed different bills, still it may really be considered as a single Act.

As before mentioned, at the renewal of the charter in 1833, the Government reserved the power of declaring the exclusive privileges of the Bank of England at an end in 1844. In the month of April of that year a correspondence was opened by Mr. Goulburn, the Chancellor of the Exchequer, with the Governor and Deputy-Governor of the Bank as to the new enactments proposed by the ministry; to which, after ineffectual efforts on the part of the Bank to obtain better terms as regards the amount to be paid in lieu of stamp duty, the consent of the court of directors was given.

The main object in view in these changes was 'to place the general circulation of the country on a sounder footing, and to prevent as much as possible fluctuations in the currency, of the nature

of those which have at different times occasioned
hazard to the Bank, and embarrassment to the
country.' *

As to the success of the means employed to
attain this end opinions vary greatly, and the
names on either side of the question are of very
high authority. Want of space prevents the arguments being fully stated here : suffice it to remark
that the advocates of the Act have a *primâ facie*
case against them, inasmuch as neither in 1847,
1857, nor 1866, did it, *when in operation, prevent* the
panic, although *when suspended* a better state of
feeling immediately arose.†

The clauses of the Act relative to the Bank of
England are as follows :—1st. That on and after
the 31st August, 1844, the issue of bank-notes
payable on demand by the Bank of England should
be separated and thenceforth kept wholly distinct
from the general banking business, and should be
carried on by a separate department, entitled
'The Issue Department of the Bank of England.'

2nd. That on the 31st August, 1844, there should
be transferred to the Issue Department securities
to the value of 14,000,000*l.* (of which the debt

* Mr. Goulburn's Letter, April 16, 1844.
† Vide extract from the 'Times.' Appendix.

due by the public should be deemed a part), and also any gold and silver not required for banking purposes; and thereupon the Issue Department should deliver to the Banking Department such an amount of notes as should, together with those in the hands of the public, be exactly equal to the aggregate amount of securities, gold, and silver transferred to the Issue Department. The Bank was forbidden to increase the securities in the Issue Department, but it might decrease them at pleasure, and again increase them up to the limit.

After the transfer the Issue Department could only issue notes in exchange for other notes, or for gold and silver coin or bullion, either to the banking department or the public generally.

3rd. That the silver bullion held by the Issue Department should not at any time exceed one fourth part of the gold coin and bullion.

4th. That after August 31, 1844, all persons should be entitled to demand notes for standard gold, at the rate of 3l. 17s. 9d. per ounce, the assay to be conducted by persons approved by the Bank, and the expense thereof to be borne by the seller.

5th. That if any banker, who on May 6, 1844, was issuing his own notes, should cease to do so, it should be lawful for the Privy Council, on the application of the Bank of England, to authorise the increase of the securities in the Issue Department beyond 14,000,000*l.*, by a sum not exceeding two-thirds of the issue so discontinued, and thereupon to issue notes to that amount; the authority for so doing to be published in the next ' Gazette.'

6th. That the accounts of the Bank should be published weekly in the ' London Gazette.'

7th. That Bank of England notes should be freed from stamp duty.

8th. That the sum paid by the Bank for its exclusive privileges should be raised from 120,000*l.* to 180,000*l.* per annum; and all profits arising from increased issues (under clause 5) should be paid to the public.

9th. That it should be lawful for the Bank, up to August 1, 1856, to compound with banks of issue to discontinue their own notes, and substitute those of the Bank at the rate of 1 per cent. per annum, the amount of such composition to be deducted from the sum paid by the Bank to the public.

10th. That the Bank of England should retain all privileges not abolished by this Act till twelve months' notice had been received by the Bank, which notice might be given after August 1, 1855, and after repayment by the public of all debts due to the Bank.

The authorised circulation has, in accordance with the provisions of the fifth clause, been thrice increased: viz. in December 1855, 475,000*l.*; July 1861, 175,000*l.*; January 1866, 350,000*l.*, which brings the fixed issue of the Bank, exclusive of that against bullion and coin, to 15,000,000*l.*

The clauses in the Act of 1844 respecting country banks are also of great importance; they are as follows :—

1st. That no person other than a banker who on May 6, 1844, was issuing his own notes, should, after the passing of the Act, have the power to do so in any part of the United Kingdom.

2nd. That after the passing of the Act it should not be lawful for any banker to draw, accept, make, or issue in England or Wales any bill of exchange, promissory note, or engagement for the payment of money to bearer on demand, or to borrow, owe, or take up any sums of money on the bills or notes of such banker payable to bearer on demand, except such bankers as were on May 6, 1844, issuing their own notes, who should, under restrictions hereafter named, continue to do so. The rights of any existing firm should not be affected by the admission or retirement of partners, provided the number did not exceed six.

3rd. That if a bank of issue should discontinue issuing, whether from bankruptcy or other cause, it should not be lawful to resume.

4th. That every banker claiming to issue notes should give notice to the Commissioners of Stamps and Taxes, the place, name, and firm, at and under which he had issued notes during the twelve weeks preceding April 27, 1844. That the average amount in circulation for those twelve weeks should be ascertained, and it should then be lawful for the bank to continue to issue notes, provided that on an average of four weeks the certified sum should not be exceeded.

5th. That if during the twelve weeks preceding April 27, 1844, two banks of issue had amalgamated, it should be lawful for the united bank to issue notes to the aggregate amount of each separate bank.

6th. That the Commissioners of Taxes should publish in the ' Gazette ' a statement of the authorised issue of each bank.

7th. That if, after the passing of the Act, two banks amalgamated, the aggregate amount of the

notes of each separate bank should be the authorised amount of the united bank, provided the total number of partners did not exceed six, in which case the privilege of issuing notes should cease.

8th. That if, on an average of four weeks, it should appear that any banker had exceeded his authorised issue, he should forfeit a sum equal to the excess.

9th. That every bank of issue should make a weekly return to the Commissioners of Taxes of the amount of notes in circulation each day of the week, and every four weeks of the *average* amount during that time, these returns to be published in the 'Gazette.' A false return to be punished by a fine of 100*l*.

10th. That the average should not exceed the amount certified by the Commissioners.

11th. That the Commissioners should have the power to examine and make extracts from bankers' books.

12th. That every banker should, on January 1 in each year, forward to the Commissioners aforesaid the name, residence, and occupation of each member of the firm, which particulars should be published in the local newspapers.

13th. That banks of issue having branches should be required to take out a licence for each branch, with this exception, that banks in existence prior to this Act, and having already four licences, should not be required to increase that number.

14th. That after the passing of the Act, it should be lawful for any number of persons, though exceeding six, carrying on the business of banking in London, or within sixty-five miles thereof, to draw, accept, or indorse bills of exchange, not being payable to bearer on demand, any Acts to the contrary notwithstanding.

It strikes one at once on reading over this Act, that the great means to the end of 'placing the general circulation of the country on a sounder footing,' in the opinion of Sir Robert Peel, was to sweep away all banks of issue except one, which was to be tied down to an arbitrary amount under all circumstances, as, of course, the exchange of notes for gold is no increase to the currency, but simply a convenience to the public.

It would seem, indeed, that it was no feeling of consideration for the country banking interest which procured it terms even as advantageous as these ; on the contrary, a fear that hostility on the

part of the bankers would endanger the success of
the measure, and, possibly, the knowledge that it
would cause considerable inconvenience in the
country, was the reason of the leniency shown
by Sir Robert Peel to the banks of issue; otherwise he would probably have finished at once
what will now be a work of time; viz. the extinc-
tion of the country note issue.

Sir Robert Peel avowed his own predilection for
a central bank of issue, and it appears from his
tone that he would have preferred the establishment of a new bank for the purpose, under the
auspices of Government.

In the speech he made at the introduction of
this measure, ho laid great stress on the evils
of uncontrolled competition amongst banks of
issue, and adduced the American banks as an instance of the truth of his views; but, singularly
enough, overlooked the Scotch banks, which were
entirely unrestrained, and of whose solvency and
respectability there was no question.

Banking authorities are almost unanimous in
asserting that with a note circulation convertible
into gold on demand it is impossible to force it
beyond the requirements of trade, for it will
be either returned in exchange for gold or be

made a deposit, but certainly in some way returned to the issuer.

The following figures will show the effect of the Act of 1844 on the issues of country notes. At the passing of the Act there were in England and Wales, issuing notes :—

204 Private Banks with authorised issues amounting to . . . . . }	£5,153,407
72 Joint-Stock Banks	3,495,116
	£8,648,863

Of these the following have, from a variety of causes, discontinued their issues :—

71 Private Banks with authorised issues amounting to . . . . . }	£1,089,895
15 Joint-Stock Banks	719.632
	£1,809,527

Leaving the fixed issues of the country banks at present (May, 1866) as follows :—

133 Private Banks with authorised issues of	£1,063,512
57 Joint-Stock Banks	2,775,814
	£6,839,326

In practice no bank can keep up to its fixed issue for fear of being in excess on the average of four weeks; when banks have numerous branches the amount reserved is necessarily a large proportion.

The Bills regulating the Irish and Scotch banks were not passed until 1845, and are materially different in their provisions to the one just described.

The only legal tender in the sister countries is gold.

Irish and Scotch banks have the privilege of issuing notes as small as 1*l.* Like the English banks they have fixed issues. In practice there is this difference, that whilst in England the limit cannot be exceeded, in Ireland and Scotland it can, if the bank has gold and silver to the amount of the excess. Weekly returns are made as in England, but the large and small notes must be divided, and the total of gold and silver shown.

In Ireland there are six banks of issue, whose fixed issues amount to 6,354,494*l.*

In Scotland there are thirteen banks of issue, and their total issue is 2,749,271*l.*

The fixed issues of the United Kingdom are at present (May, 1866) :—

Bank of England	£15,000,000
English Private Banks	4,063,512
„ Joint-Stock Banks	2,775,814
Irish Banks	6,354,494
Scotch Banks	2,749,271
Total . .	£30,943,091

Passing from the consideration of this important
Act of Parliament, it becomes necessary to make
some few reflections prompted by the facts, and
shortly to notice the various opinions and theories
respecting the proper regulation required on the
one hand to secure the convertibility of the note,
and on the other to keep the issues within due
bounds. Intimately connected with these two
points, is the arrangement necessary to insure
an adequate supply of the precious metals. In
entering upon the consideration of this most important element in our financial system, it is well
to remark that however great may be the present
necessity that the paper currency of this kingdom
should be based securely, and conducted on the
soundest principles, the question is not of that
vital importance to the country that it was a
century ago, when it would have been thought
impossible to have carried on the business of a
banker without having a large note issue. We
now see many of the greatest banks in every
sense of the word who have never issued notes,
and some of the most prosperous who have done
so discontinuing the practice; thus clearly showing that it is by no means essential to the prosperity of a banker to have the privilege. Largely

as the trade of this country has increased in all
its branches, it is a fact well known to all connected with financial matters, that the note circulation slowly but certainly diminishes; a fact
suggesting rather a singular reflection, and showing the fallacy of the ideas that were generally
received on the subject. The decrease of that
branch of banking which last century was deemed
the most important, may now be taken as a very
good proof of the enormous increase of the business in general. Doubtless it will be argued by
many that, as regards the country bank-notes,
this is the effect of the legislative measures of
1844, and to a certain extent that view may be
accepted as correct; but if the returns in the
'Gazette' be examined, it will be found that many
bankers are always below their authorised issues
by from 25 to 50 per cent., some even more.

These remarks are by no means intended to
imply that the proper regulation of the paper
currency is of secondary importance; and, later, it
will be desirable to consider whether some improvement might not be made on our present
system.

Fifty or sixty years ago it was no uncommon
opinion that a circulating medium of any descrip-

tion, save and except the precious metals, was vicious in principle. Of late years only one writer. (we believe) has gone to this length; he, however, in a work, published within the last twenty years, evidently considers paper currency and the pressure of the national debt to be evils so gigantic, that nothing short of the abolition of the one and the repudiation of the other will redeem the hopeless condition of the nation—'once high-spirited, happy, rich, free, and great, brought down to the state of a set of spiritless, half-starved, corrupted, and bewildered slaves by a body of usurers and villains as contemptible as any that ever made the sun blush to shine upon them, or the winds of heaven unable to blow over them without nausea and loathing.'

The theories that have at different times been started as to the right and proper regulations that should govern a paper currency, have been almost as numerous as the writers on the subject. There is the celebrated theory of Mr. Law, that notes may be safely issued by the owners of land or commodities, to the value of such property; and truly it is a most taking idea, it having been tried in France, America, and in our own country, and has always ended disastrously, when pushed to its

logical conclusion. The only reason for noticing
it here is to point out that in a modified form we
have it still in force. The Act of 1844 gives the
Bank of England the power of considering that
portion of its capital which has been lent to the
Government, and over which it has lost all control,
as a part of the security on which the issues of
notes are based. It is true that, going as it
does, to a limited extent, no danger to the community can possibly arise, still the principle is the
same as that advocated by Mr. Law.

It has been thought that an extension of note
issues had the same effect on the country that an
influx of the precious metals had, and in the case
of an *inconvertible* paper currency, for a time it
does seem to have that effect; as notes are
issued prices rise rapidly, and all seem getting
rich until time proves such a notion to be entirely
fallacious.

It would be simply a waste of space to argue
for, or attempt to show the advantages of, an inconvertible paper currency, public opinion in this
country having so emphatically decided that it
should be convertible ; and legislation following in
its wake, has done what was possible to ensure this
absolutely, so far as Bank of England notes are

P

concerned, by fixing the price at which gold can
be demanded at the Bank in exchange for notes.
In the case of country bankers in England and
Wales, their issues may be based on either gold or
Bank of England notes, the inability to furnish
either in exchange for their own notes being
deemed proof of bankruptcy.

To secure the absolute convertibility of the note,
it is necessary that there should be a basis of
bullion, and so long as a due proportion between
the issues and the precious metals is preserved, so
long is convertibility ensured.

Parliament thought it impossible that under any
circumstances the Bank of England notes in the
hands of the public could fall below 14,000,000l.,
and therefore only required the amount beyond
that to be secured by bullion. But as matters
now stand, the Bank issues 15,000,000l. against
securities, thus showing that the authorised
country issues have since 1844 been diminished by at least 1,500,000l., though practically
the reduction is much more considerable. It is,
therefore, a very fair subject for consideration,
whether the fixed issue of the Bank of England
might not be advantageously increased, still at
present the balance of opinion is certainly in

favour of the present limit, although at every
recurrence of 'tightness' in the money market, an
outcry is raised that it is owing to the restrictions
on the Bank.

As to the sum either in Bank paper or coin
required to protect country issues, the legislature
has left the bankers entirely to their own discretion, and it hardly seems possible to fix a uniform
proportion for the whole kingdom, some districts
being much more liable to large and sudden
demands than others.

Sir Archibald Alison, in his 'History of Europe,'
considers that the circulating medium (i.e. coin
and notes) should as much as possible be kept to
a fixed amount, that when gold is exported notes
should be issued to supply its place; if bullion be
imported notes should be withdrawn from circulation. But then the difficulty arises, if gold
be exported and the vacuum supplied by paper,
and the rate of interest not at the same time
raised, in all probability the drain will continue,
and in course of time the convertibility of the note
would be endangered, if not destroyed. Moreover,
with a brisk trade a larger amount of the circulating medium is required than at a time when
commerce is languishing, so that the dead level

which Sir Archibald advocates is scarcely desirable. To a certain extent, in ordinary times, his
object is attained by the arrangement prohibiting
the Bank of England from issuing notes beyond
a fixed limit, unless an equal amount of gold be
withdrawn from circulation; but on the occasions
since this restrictive enactment has been in force,
when serious monetary panics have taken place,
as in the autumn of 1847, and 1857, it has been
found to intensify existing evils, and has been
temporarily suspended with the best possible
results.* The friends of the Act of 1844 say, and
say truly, that neither in 1847 nor 1857 was the
convertibility of the note endangered; but when
they attempt to show that this was a result of
Sir Robert Peel's Act their case at once breaks
down. Convertibility was as safe before as after
the passing of that Act; the directors of the
Bank of England would have been in care to
provide for that, whoever might have suffered in
the effort. But supposing that through any chain
of circumstances, at the periods in question, the
bank-note had fallen into discredit, how would the
case have then stood? When the suspensions of
the Act of 1844 took place in 1847 and 1857 the

* Vide Appendix.

state of things in the Issue Department was as follows :—

Octobrr 23, 1847.
Notes in the hands of the public	. £21,000,000
Bullion	. 7,866,000

November 12, 1857.
Notes in the hands of the public	. . £21,000,000
Bullion	6,524,000

thus showing that the *absolute* inconvertibility of the note was not secured.

But if the Issue Department was not safe, how did the Banking Department stand?

October 23, 1847.
Private Deposits . .	. . £8,580,000
Notes and Coin in reserve .	. . 2,094,000

November 12, 1857.
Private Deposits	. £12,935,000
Notes and Coin in reserve . .	. 1,461,000

Now, looking at these figures, although it is very clear that if gold had been demanded at the counter in the ' Hall ' for more than a third of the notes in circulation the demand could not have been supplied, practically no danger was to be apprehended on this head, for the public were only too anxious to get the notes; but there was a real and tangible danger to the banking department—so great, indeed, that had not the Government intervened, a suspension of payment must

have taken place, although millions of bullion
were in the vaults; and will any one seriously
affirm that this would not have been a disaster, by
the side of which the temporary inconvertibility
of the note would have been mere child's play,
entailing as it would have done the absolute suspension of business throughout the country?

There seems to be a strong feeling that it is
necessary to restrain the Bank of England, and,
indeed, all the banks of issue, from abusing their
privileges by stringent regulations, but a very
great diversity of opinion exists as to the best
means of attaining that object. It has been proposed that the Bank of England should not be
controlled directly in its issues, but that it should
adopt a graduated rate of interest founded on the
amount of notes in circulation, and bullion in the
vaults. There are, however, so many points to
be taken into consideration in deciding upon
raising or lowering the rate of interest, that it
seems very unjust to tie the hands of the directors
in so important a particular; it would greatly
impede them in their duties to both the holders of
bank stock, and also to their customers. Moreover, in proposing such an arrangement, there is
involved the assumption of a fallacy that the Bank

of England has the command of the rate of
interest, which it most undoubtedly has not; that
institution, like any other, must follow the market;
if the rate out of doors be 5 per cent. it would be
simply childish of the directors to fix their rate at
6 per cent.; the only effect of such a course would
be to diminish the dividend on Bank Stock, because, although notes would flow in as securities
ran off, they would be drawn out again through the
depositors. It may, perhaps, be said that the rate
of interest outside the Bank of England corre-
sponds to the terms exacted by that establishment;
but the fact that it does so only proves that the
opinion of the public coincides with that of the
Bank directors.

Of course, in fixing the rate of interest, the
amount of the reserve of notes and bullion is a
most important element, not only as to the resources of the Bank, but as a monetary barometer
showing the state of the atmosphere of the money
market. Still it will not do to treat a foreign
drain of gold in the same way as a domestic one,
the latter being invariably of a special, and generally of a temporary nature.

In a most able article published in ' Blackwood's
Magazine ' for March 1866, well worthy of the

attentive perusal of all interested in this and
kindred subjects, the writer strongly deprecates
the obligation imposed on the Bank of keeping
the security for the notes in the form of bullion.
He argues most justly and forcibly that a drain of
gold does not take place through the Issue Department, and that the only demands for gold through
that department are for the supply of small change.
He therefore proposes that the Issue Department
should transfer the bullion to the Banking Department, receiving Government securities in exchange, and that in future notes should be issued
entirely against such securities. The effect of
this would be to increase the strength of the
reserve in the Banking Department to an enormous extent, as the whole of the bullion would
be available.   There remains the question whether
if that were so, the temptation to allow this unprofitable portion of their assets to fall to a low
figure, and thereby increase the profits of the
Bank, might not be too great for the virtue of
the authorities.

It is here as well to remark a slight error into
which the writer of the article in ' Blackwood '
has fallen: he speaks of the depositors at the
Bank having an equal claim on the bullion in the

Issue Department as the holders of notes, which is clearly contrary to the spirit and letter of the Act of Parliament.

Respecting the issues of country notes, there being no security whatever provided for them, it seems that it would be but an act of justice to declare that in cases of bankruptcy, the holders of notes should have their claims settled before the depositors or other creditors.

With reference to the larger part of the question, the regulation of Bank of England issues, the space prescribed to this branch being exhausted, it must suffice to say that for fair weather the Act of 1844 works, or rather leaves other things to work, tolerably well; but in times of commercial panic it is more than questionable whether it does not aggravate and intensify existing evils.

CHAPTER X.

OF COINS.

THE earliest mention that is made in authentic
history of the use of a metal currency occurs in
the 23rd chapter of Genesis, where Abraham
bought the field of Macpelah for 400 shekels of
silver—one shekel was about 2s. 3½d. A talent was
3,000 shekels, or 342l. 3s. 9d.; a talent of gold,
5,475l.—both Jewish. With whom the talent
originated, or when, is not recorded. The Jews
were in the habit in those times of weighing their
money in scales, which they carried about with
them for the purpose. The earliest mention of
coins is made in 1 Chron. xxix. 7, and Ezra, ii. 69,
where the Persian coin, the daric, is spoken of,
which was of gold, value 2s., having an impression
on one side of an archer kneeling. Gold was
used by the Egyptians before silver—the latter
was called by them white gold; both metals were
afterwards used for their currency, being made up

in the form of rings, without, however, any stamp
or indication of their purity or weight ; these rings
were generally weighed in the gross against other
weights in the shape of oxen and lambs, which
tedious process continued as late as the time of
the Ptolemies, and was only gradually superseded
by Grecian coins. It is recorded that Aryandes,
Governor of Egypt, struck silver coins in imitation
of the golden ones of the Persian empire, for
which invasion of prerogative the king struck off
his head. On the Persians quitting the country
these coins were discontinued. The earliest mention of a coin with any pretension to a value of its
own stamped upon it was the Lydian ' stater,' a
Greek coin, a mixture of gold and silver, as three
to one. They were simply lumps of metal struck
on one side only, leaving the impression of a lion's
head or other emblem. Darius was the first to
introduce coins of real gold, though it would seem
that they were intended as medals, and afterwards used as coins. The ring money before
spoken of was circulating in Britain previous to
the invasion of the Romans. We learn from
Cæsar that the Gauls also used iron and gold rings
of certain weights for their money. The gold
rings have been discovered at no distant date in

Ireland. These Irish rings possessed much more
the features of a true coinage than the pieces of
metal used by the Egyptians, as the larger ones
have been found on being weighed to be multiples of
the small ones or units. The Roman coinage ceased
in Britain, and was succeeded by the Saxon on the
Romans leaving the country, A.D. 426. Herodotus
gives Pheidon, King of Argos, the credit of having
first introduced weights, measures, and coins into
Greece, the coins having been struck at Ægina,
being also lumps of metal like the Lydian, with
the impression of a turtle or tortoise stamped on
one side. Silver was the only currency in Greece
until the time of Crœsus, who is said to have given
Alcmæon as much gold as he could carry. The
gold coinage of Persia and other nations circulated at Athens until the time of Alexander the
Great, when both gold and copper coins became
common. The most worthless currency of which
we find record was that of Sparta, where the
native iron, so tempered as to be useless for any
other purpose, was formed into little bars and
employed as legal currency; also leather is said to
have been used for the same purpose. This extraordinary proceeding seems to have originated with
Lycurgus, who having travelled much in other

countries, was at length recalled to quell the feuds in his own. Having convinced himself, like many modern philosophers, that money was the root of all evil, he conceived the idea of prohibiting the use of gold and silver to his countrymen, and we find that up to the latest age of the state it was forbidden to any Spartan to possess gold or silver. The Hollanders used pasteboard as late as 1574. On renouncing all such articles as leather and shells, countries will be found to have adopted the metals most easily obtainable. The Greeks used silver; the Egyptians gold; Italy copper, &c., and they stamped them with a device representing wealth, such as cattle and sheep—whence *pecunia* and the Greek coin βοῦς. The florin also from fiorino, the Florentine lily. The original Roman coin was the 'as,' which as time wore on they reduced from 12 oz. to 1 oz., whereby they reduced their debt in a like proportion.

Having thus briefly touched upon ancient money and coins, simply as an introduction to the coinage of Great Britain, we shall pass on to the time of Athelstan, A.D. 925. Should the foregoing remarks create a desire in the reader to become familiar with the coinages and articles used formerly as money in other countries, we can

recommend the work entitled ' Ruding's Annals of
the Coinage,' published about the year 1840 or
1841, and for silver coins only, ' Hawkins on the
Silver Coinage ' (the latter of England only).

Here follows the coinage of England from Athelstan, A.D. 925, to Victoria, for which we are much
indebted to W. S. W. Vaux, Esq., M.A., &c. &c., of
the British Museum, and President of the Numis-
matic Society.

The denominations only of the coins are given
as they were issued in the different reigns :—

Coinage of England.

Athelstan, A.D. 925, to Henry II., A.D. 1189, silver pennies only.

Richard I.			No English money.
John			No English money.
Henry III.	*Gold*	Pennies.	
"	*Silver*	Pennies.	
Edward I.	*Silver*	Groats, pennies, halfpennies, far-	
		things.	
Edward II. . . .	*Silver*	Pennies, halfpennies.	
Edward III. . . .	*Gold*	Florin, half-florin, quarter-florin,	
		noble, half-noble, quarter-noble.	
"	*Silver*	Groat, half-groat, penny, halfpenny,	
		farthing.	
Richard II. . . .	*Gold*	Noble, half-noble, quarter-noble.	
"	*Silver*	Groat, half-groat, penny, halfpenny,	
		farthing.	
Henry IV.	*Gold*	Noble, half-noble.	
"	*Silver*	Groat, penny, halfpenny.	
Henry V.			No English money.
Henry VI.	*Gold*	Angel, angelet.	
"	*Silver*	Groat, penny, halfpenny.	

Henry IV. V. or VI.	*Gold*	Noble, half-noble, quarter-noble.
„	*Silver*	Groat, half-groat, penny, halfpenny, farthing.
Edward IV. . . .	*Gold*	Rose-noble, half-noble, quarter-noble, angel, angelet.
„	*Silver*	Groat, half-groat, penny, halfpenny, farthing.
Edward V.	*Gold*	Angel, angolet.
„	*Silver*	None.
Richard III. . . .	*Gold*	Angel, angelet.
„	*Silver*	Groat, half-groat, penny, halfpenny, farthing.
Henry VII. . . .	*Gold*	Sovereign, rose-noble, angel, angelet.
„	*Silver*	Shilling, groat, half-groat, penny, halfpenny, farthing.
Henry VIII. . . .	*Gold*	Sovereign, half-sovereign, rose-noble, crown, half-crown, angel, half-angel, quarter-angel, George-noble.
„	*Silver*	Shilling, groat, half-groat, penny, halfpenny, farthing.
Edward VI. . . .	*Gold*	Three-pound piece, sovereign, double-sovereign, half-sovereign, quarter-sovereign, half-crown, angel.
„	*Silver*	Shilling, groat, half-groat, crown, half-crown, penny, halfpenny, farthing.
Mary	*Gold*	Sovereign, royal, angel, half-angel.
„	*Silver*	Half-crown, shilling, sixpence, groat, half-groat, penny.
Philip and Mary . .	*Gold*	None.
„	*Silver*	Half-crown.
Elizabeth	*Gold*	Sovereign, pound-sovereign, half-pound, quarter-pound, half-quarter pound, royal, angel, half-angel, quarter-angel.
	Silver	Crown, half-crown, shilling, groat, half-groat, penny, sixpence, three-pence, twopence, three halfpence, three farthings.

James I.	*Gold*	Rose-royal, spur-royal, angel, half-angel, pound-sovereign, unite, laurel, half-sovereign, half-unite, double-crown, half-laurel, quarter-sovereign, Britain-crown, quarter-laurel, thistle-crown, half-crown.
„	*Silver*	Half-groat, shilling, sixpence, half-crown, crown.
„	*Copper*	Pennies.
Charles I.	*Gold*	Three-pound piece, angel, unite, double-crown, British-crown.
	Silver	Twenty-shilling piece, crown, half-crown, shilling, sixpence, groat, threepence, half-groat.
„	*Copper*	Pennies.
Oliver Cromwell . .	*Gold*	None.
„	*Silver*	Crown, half-crown.
„	*Copper*	Farthing.
Commonwealth . .	*Gold*	Unite, half-unite, crown.
„	*Silver*	Crown, half-crown, shilling, sixpence, half-groat.
Charles II.	*Gold*	Twenty-shilling piece, double-crown, crown, five-guinea piece, two-guinea, one-guinea, half-guinea.
„	*Silver*	Crown, half-crown, shilling, sixpence, fourpence, threepence, twopence.
„	*Copper*	Halfpenny, farthing.
James II.	*Gold*	Five-guinea, two-guinea, one-guinea, half-guinea.
	Silver	Crown, half-crown, shilling, sixpence, fourpence, threepence, twopence.
„	*Copper*	Halfpenny, farthing.
William and Mary .	*Gold*	Five-guinea, two-guinea, one-guinea, half-guinea.
	Silver	Crown, half-crown, shilling, sixpence, fourpence, threepence, twopence.
	Copper	Halfpence, farthing.

William III. . . . *Gold* Five-guinea, two-guinea, one-guinea, half-guinea.

" *Silver* Crown, half-crown, shilling, sixpence, fourpence, threepence, twopence.

" *Copper* Farthing.

Anne . . . . . . *Gold* Five-guinea, two-guinea, one-guinea, half-guinea.

" *Silver* Crown, half-crown, shilling, sixpence, fourpence, threepence, twopence.

" *Copper* Halfpenny, farthing.

George I. . . . . *Gold* Five-guinea, two-guinea, one-guinea, half-guinea, quarter-guinea.

" *Silver* Crown, half-crown, shilling, sixpence, fourpence, threepence, twopence.

" *Copper* Halfpence.

George II. . . . . *Gold* Five-guinea, two-guinea, one-guinea, half-guinea.

" *Silver* Crown, half-crown, shilling, sixpence, fourpence, threepence, twopence.

" *Copper* Halfpence.

George III. . . . *Gold* One-guinea, half-guinea, seven-shilling piece, quarter-guinea, sovereign, half-sovereign.

" *Silver* Crown, half-crown, shilling, sixpence, fourpence, threepence, twopence.

" *Copper* Twopence, penny, halfpenny, farthing.

George IV. . . . . *Gold* Double-sovereign, one-sovereign, half-sovereign.

" *Silver* Crown, half-crown, shilling, sixpence, fourpence, threepence, twopence.

Copper Farthing.

Q

William IV. . . .	*Gold*	Sovereign, half-sovereign.
"	*Silver*	Crown, half-crown, shilling, sixpence, fourpence, threepence, twopence.
"	*Copper*	None.
Victoria	*Gold*	Sovereign, half-sovereign.
"	*Silver*	Crown, half-crown, florin, shilling, sixpence, fourpence, threepence.
"	*Copper*	Penny, halfpenny, farthing.
"	*Bronze* (1860)	Penny, halfpenny, farthing.

Athelstan, we are informed, was the first to establish uniform coin in England, and after that time the kings became the bullion merchants and coiners.

The royal mint was established in the reign of Edward II. There were also several provincial mints under the control of that of London. Henry II. instituted one at Winchester, 1125. Stow informs us the mint was kept by Italians, the English being ignorant of the art of coining, 7 Edward I., 1278. The operators were formed into a corporation by charter of Edward III. The first entry of gold into the mint for coinage purposes occurred 18 Edward III., 1343. Tin was coined by Charles II., 1684; gun metal and pewter by his successor, James. The present mint, for the erection of which grants were made between 1806 and 1810 to the amount of 262,000*l*., was partially destroyed by fire in 1815. The new constitution of the mint took effect in 1817. The mint has eight melting furnaces, two cranes, and two pouring machines. The furnaces are used three times a day when coining is going on, and as each pot is about 420 pounds, they melt 10,080 pounds in a day of ten hours. The gold pots are about 100 pounds, and melt it in an hour. The gold bars are rolled cold to the thickness of the coin, and the silver bars hot. The old hammer and punch were superseded by the mill and screw in the reign of Queen Elizabeth, to whose ministers we are greatly indebted for the restoration of the coinage. They also stamped the coins with their true value, so that persons who held the debased coins lost about five-sixths by such operation, for which they had mainly to thank Henry VIII., during whose reign the currency had been allowed to sink to such a degraded state. The number of coins issuing from the mint each year varies considerably according to circumstances, such as depreciation by abrasion, &c.

We subjoin the gold, silver, and copper or bronze coinages for the four years from 1859 to 1862, taken from the statistical abstract presented by command to both Houses of Parliament:—

Years.	Gold.	Silver.	Copper or Bronze.	Total.
1859	2,649,500	647,064	8,512	3,305,085
1860	3,121,700	218,403	37,990	3,378,102
1861	8,190,170	200,484	273,578	8,673,232
1862	7,836,413	148,518	352,800	8,337,731

The gold coins at present in use in Great Britain
are, first, the £ sterling or sovereign. £ signifies
pounds, from the Latin 'libræ;' sterling is the
contraction of easterling, and is supposed to have
been first adopted in the reign of Henry VII., being
derived from the festival of Easter,* when Government officials visited the Mint and examined
the coinage. The sovereign was first minted by
Henry VII., and was then a 20s. piece. Twenty-
two and a half of these pieces were coined from the
pound tower; and the pound tower containing 5,400
grains, there were 240 grains of gold in each
coin. The sovereign at present in use contains
113·12 grains of pure gold, so that the sovereign
of Henry VII. was intrinsically worth 2l. 2s. 5d. of
our money. On July 1, 1817, a coin in imitation
of the one coined by Henry VII. was proclaimed

* Easter is derived from 'Eastra,' the Saxon goddess, whose
festival fell in April.

current, and to be of the value of 20s., called a
sovereign. It weighed 5 dwts. 3·274 grs. of standard gold.* Henry VIII. debased the gold coin
from 23 carats 3½ grs. fine, with ½ gr. of alloy, to
22 carats pure and 2 of alloy. He also debased
the silver to 4 oz. fine and 8 of alloy; that is to
say, by successive stages during his reign it reached
that debased state.

Two neighbouring kingdoms, Scotland and
France, we find were even in a worse condition.
The pound Scots had become reduced to $\frac{1}{36}$ part of
its original value. The pound weight, which is
now coined into 66 shillings, was coined into 144
shillings in the year 1475; and from that, by gradual reductions or debasements, was coined into
720 in 1601. The French, we find, were still worse
than the Scotch, judging from an extract taken
from the Mint Indenture of Edward I. Their
'sou,' corrupted from 'solidus,' meaning a shilling,
now represents a halfpenny of our money; the
'livre' nearly corresponded to the modern franc at
the termination of the old monarchy.

* On Saturday, Feb. 3, 1866, at a privy council, it was ordered
that the sovereign of the Sydney mint, in Australia, should be proclaimed a legal tender in this country, and in all British possessions.
In Mauritius and Ceylon it has for some time been legal currency,
and it will now have imperial circulation.

The standard purity of the sovereign underwent many changes until fixed by James I. at 22 carats as the standard purity, which has remained without alteration up to the present time. The carat is the 24th part of a pound troy, or 10 dwts.; and the carat grain, 2 dwts. 12 grs. troy. The legal weight of the sovereign is 5 dwts. 2¾ grs. The half-sovereign was coined also on July 1, 1817, and what has been said of the sovereign with respect to weight and fineness applies to it also. Of the silver coinage, the florin, shilling, sixpenny piece, and threepenny piece, are to remain permanently in circulation until some further decimal change takes place. The crown or five-shilling piece, the half-crown and fourpenny piece, are no longer coined, and only remain in circulation until they are so defaced that the Bank will be compelled to withdraw them. The florin, as we have before observed, derives its name from 'fiorino,' the Florentine lily; this is the only alteration since 1817 (with the exception of the bronze coinage) that has taken place, and was coined with the intention of introducing the decimal system.

In 1503 (the 18th of Henry VII.) the old Saxon money of account, the shilling, was converted into a coin. It contained 144 grains of silver; and, as

our modern shilling contains 80·7 grains, it was
intrinsically worth 1*s.* 9·408*d.* of our money. The
Irish shilling was struck in 1560. English and
Irish money was assimilated January 1, 1826. The
weight of a shilling is 3 dwts. 15₁⁹₁ grs. The groat
is derived from 'grot,' which signifies great, it
being the largest of the Saxon coins then in use.
The division of the pound into 20*s.*, and the shilling
into 12 pence, was introduced by William the
Conqueror after the plan of Charlemagne in France
in the eighth century, and is supposed to be derived
from the Romans. The ancient silver penny is
said to have been the first silver coin in use among
the Anglo-Saxons. It was coined with a cross
deeply indented, so that it might be broken in
two or four pieces. This peculiarity ceased with
Edward I.

Charles I. issued silver coins of 7¼ grs., called
silver pennies, of the same weight and purity as
those issued by his father. This coin was not
circulated after the Restoration of Charles II. The
lowest silver coin struck after this silver penny was
the sixpence. The silver coins are not now legal
tender for sums above 40 shillings. The coins
smaller than this were used for Maunday money.
The Maunday money consisted of 4, 3, 2, and

1 penny pieces in silver, which were distributed
among the poor the Thursday before Good Friday;
called Maunday Thursday from *mande*, signifying
a hand-basket, from which the alms are supposed to
have been distributed. Another authority says,
from 'dies mandati,' as the day when Christ gave
His great 'mandate' that we should love one
another. This custom was begun by Edward III.,
A.D. 1363, when he was 50 years of age. On this
day it was the custom of our kings or their almo-
ners to relieve as many old men as they were years
old. The custom still exists.

The copper coinage of England cannot be said to
have existed until the reign of Queen Elizabeth.
The want of a smaller coin than the silver penny
caused the importation of large quantities of base
coin from the continent for the convenience of
people in trade, whose only means of using a part
of the silver penny was by breaking it into two
or four, which the cross deeply indented in the
coin admitted of their doing. In the reign of
Henry VIII., however, the traders being perplexed
for want of small coins, commenced issuing private
tokens of lead to represent halfpence and farthings.
This went on through the succeeding reigns until
the ministers of Elizabeth thought that a national

coinage of copper would be far preferable to this
endless and confusing variety of tokens. The
attempt failed, however; and, being revived in the
reign of James I., failed again, as far as coining
copper at the Royal Mint was concerned, and
patents were granted to private persons. At length,
in the year 1672, a coinage of copper took place at
the Royal Mint. Nothing of any importance inter-
fered with the copper coinage until December 1860,
when the bronze coinage was introduced. The
bronze coinage of 1861 (the first full year after its
introduction) weighed 665 tons, and consisted of
pence, halfpence, and farthings, to the number of
99 millions. The material of which it is composed
consists of 95 parts of copper, 4 of tin, and 1 of
zinc. Pence or halfpence are not legal tender for
more than 12d., or farthings for more than 6d.: d,
signifying pence, is derived from ‘denarii.’

The coinage of England, although superintended
by Government officers (and any alterations that
may be made are sanctioned by Parliament), is not
issued by the Government. The Bank of England
supplies the Government with bullion, as it would
any other individual, for coinage purposes. The
Bank of England has been for years the only importer of bullion into the Mint. It is, therefore,

hardly to be expected that the Bank or the Government, without the full concurrence of the country, would supply new and full-weight coin for those that have by circulation, and often ill-treatment, fallen below their legal weight. The Bank of England is compelled to meet this expense by charging the person tendering the light gold, at the rate of 4d. for the sovereign and 3d. for the half-sovereign; and is under a contract with the Government to retire from the currency the defaced silver.

The Government coins gold free of expense for any individual who sends bullion of not less than 10,000l. value; but these instances are of very rare occurrence. The whole of the coinage may be said to enter circulation through the Bank of England. The price paid for gold by the Bank is 3l. 17s. 9d. per oz., and the expense of the assay is borne by the seller. The privilege of coining silver and copper is vested solely in the Crown, who supply new coins for those retired from the currency by the Bank. The character and device of the coins of the present day are considered the prerogative of the Crown; and any impressions made afterwards by the people, by way of advertisement or otherwise, is punishable by law. It was different, however, at Rome. Each family or individual might have their own silver coined with such device as they pleased, provided its weight and purity were guaranteed by an additional stamp made by the Government officers. This was abolished by Augustus.

The guinea, now withdrawn from the currency, took its name from the country producing the gold of which it was made. It varied in value from 20 to 30 shillings till the year 1717, when, by the advice of Sir Isaac Newton, it was fixed at 21 shillings. The last coinage of guineas took place in 1813.

The system existing previous to the year 1816, which made both metals standard measures of value, caused much disorder, as they were both a legal tender to any amount. Their market prices being subject to endless variation, one or other was constantly being driven out of circulation. To remedy this, gold being the metal in which the principal payments were made, it was adopted as the standard measure of value, and the only legal tender in coin that could be made to an unlimited amount. In the same year a new coinage of sovereigns took place, in due proportion to the guinea, viz. $46\frac{1}{2}$ sovereigns to the pound troy, and of 20

shillings value each.   A new coinage of silver also
took place, when 66 shillings instead of 62 (the
old rate) were produced from the pound troy.   The
relative values of gold and silver having perceptibly
changed at the end of the eighteenth century, the
adjustment which had taken place in 1717 no
longer corresponded to the existing market value
of the metals; and consequently had a recoinage
of silver taken place at the former denomination
and weight, it must have disappeared from the
circulation as before.   To prevent this, the Government enacted that private persons should no longer
enjoy the privilege of having their silver bullion
coined; and in addition to this, the pound weight
of silver was coined into 66 shillings instead of 62,
the four shillings being kept back for the expenses
of coinage.   The present shilling, in consequence,
passes for slightly more than 6 per cent. above its
intrinsic value.   But as the public must necessarily
suffer by this arrangement, if silver were a legal
tender to any amount, a law was passed enacting
that no tender above 40s. in silver coin at one time
should be legal.   The silver coinage has since
remained entirely in the hands of the Government,
who, by judiciously limiting the quantity, have main-

tained the current value above the intrinsic value.
The circulation of silver in Great Britain and her
colonies is inconsiderable when compared with
other countries. Gold being the only metallic
legal tender for sums above 40s., the silver and
copper or bronze are simply auxiliary coins.
Wrought gold has two legal standards. The
coin is 22 carats of fine gold, mixed with 2 of
alloy; or, in other words, 8·333 alloy + 91·666
gold, which has undergone no alteration since the
reign of James I. The silver, $\frac{3}{40}$, or 7·5 alloy
+92·7 silver. The nature of the alloy is left to
the discretion of the Master of the Mint; but the
practice has always been to add copper only to
such extent as will complete the proportion of alloy,
including that which may be naturally present
in the bullion, whether gold or silver. The second
gold standard is 18 carats, mostly employed for
jewellery. Wrought silver has two legal standards.
The other standard is better than the coin, being
11 oz. 10 dwts. out of 1 pound troy.

The standard of England is gold. France has
a double standard, which causes more frequent fluctuations. The standard of most other European
countries is silver. In countries where gold is

the standard, silver in by far the largest proportion is employed as merchandise, and *vice versâ*.

The decimal coinage, about which so much discussion has taken place—some in favour of 1*l.* as the integer, some in favour of the 10*d.* integer—is, we consider, so far from a satisfactory solution, that instead of discussing the methods proposed for adoption, we must refer our readers to the pamphlets on the subject by James Laurie and others, also the opinions of a committee of the House of Commons which was in favour of the 1*l.* integer. The decimal system was introduced into France in 1790, and, according to good authorities, works most unsatisfactorily.* It is adopted in America, where the dollar is the integer; also in Holland and other countries. Sir John Wrottesley brought the subject before the British Parliament February 25, 1824. In the year 1838 a commission was appointed at the instance of the then Chancellor of the Exchequer, Mr. Spring Rice. In June 1843, another commission was appointed—both reported strongly in its favour. On August 1, 1853, a committee reported to the same effect, but Mr. Gladstone thought the change premature. Another

---

* This has reference to the weights and measures.

commission on the subject was appointed in 1855; the last discussion took place in July 1863—the result was unimportant. The decimal system was adopted in Canada January 1, 1858.

There can be no doubt existing in the mind of any advocate of social progress, or even the most conservative of modern philosophers, that the decimal coinage is in every respect the best fitted to spare the time and trouble of persons whose business involves pecuniary calculations. Having had some years' experience of the working of the decimal system of *coinage* abroad, I can without hesitation assert, that all persons who come here from a country having a decimal system, are astonished that a land whose commercial position stands so high as that of England, can continue to puzzle the brains of her sons with a system which long ago should have been but a mere matter of history.

	English	French	German	Spanish	Italian
1	one	un	ein	uno	uno
2	two	deux	zwei	dos	due
3	three	trois	drei	tres	tre
4	four	quatre	vier	cuatro	quattro
5	five	cinq	fünf	cinco	cinque
6	six	six	sechs	seis	sei
7	seven	sept	sieben	siete	sette
8	eight	huit	acht	ocho	otto
9	nine	neuf	neun	nueve	nove
10	ten	dix	zehn	diez	dieci
20	twenty	vingt	zwanzig	veinte	venti
30	thirty	trente	dreissig	treinta	trenta
40	forty	quarante	vierzig	cuarenta	quaranta
50	fifty	cinquante	fünfzig	cincuenta	cinquanta
60	sixty	soixante	sechzig	sesenta	sessanta
70	seventy	soixante-dix	siebzig	setenta	settanta
80	eighty	quatre-vingt	achtzig	ochenta	ottanta
90	ninety	quatre-vingt-dix	neunzig	noventa	novanta
100	hundred	cent	hundert	cien	cento
1000	thousand	mille	tausend	mil	mille
Day	day	jour	Tag	dia	giorno
Week	week	semaine	Woche	semana	settimana
Month	month	mois	Monat	mes	mese
Year	year	année	Jahr	año	anno
On demand	on demand	à présentation	nach Sicht, bei Vorzeigung	á presentacion	a presentazione
At sight	at sight	à vue	a vista	á la vista	a vista
After sight	after sight	à jours de vue	nach Sicht	á ... dias vista	dopo vista
After date	after date	à jours de date	nach Dato	á ... dias fecha	dopo data
Pay to the order	pay to the order	payez à l'ordre	für mich, or uns, an die Ordre	á la órden	pagate a l'ordine
I promise to pay	I promise to pay	je payeral	werde ich, or werden wir bezahlen	pagaré	pagare
With interest	with interest	avec intérêts	mit Zinsen	con interés	con interesse

Portuguese	Dutch	Russian	Turkish	Danish	Swedish
hum, m, huma, f. / dous, m. duas, f.	een twee	odun dba	bir iki	en to	en två
tres	drie	tru	utch	tre	tre
quatro	vier	tschetire	dirt	fire	fyra
cinco	vyf	piat	bech	fem	fem
seis	zes	schest	alti	sex	sex
sete	zeven	sem	yedi	syv	sju
outo	acht	votsm	skiz	otte	åtta
nove	negen	deviat	dokouz	ni	nio
dez	tien	desat	on	ti	tio
vinte	twintig	dvadzat	yirmi	tyve	tjugu
trinta	dertig	tradsat	otouz	tredive	trettio
quarenta	veertig	sorok	kirk	fyrretive	fyrtio
cincoenta	vyftig	piatdesat	elli	halvtred sindstyve	femtio
sessenta	zestig	schestdesat	altmish	tredsindstyve	sextio
setenta	zeventig	semdesat	yedmish	halvfjerds indstyve	sjuttio
oitenta	tachtig	vosemdesat	seksen	firsindstyve	åttio
noventa	negentig	devianosto	doxen	halvfems indstyve	nittio
cem	honderd	sto	yuz	hundrede	hundra
mil	duizend	tisats	bin	tusinde	tusen
dia	dag	den	gubn	dage	dag
semana	week	nedela	hafta	uger	vecka
mez	maander	mesats	ai	maaned	månad
anno	jaar	god	sêne	aar	år
á presentação	op vertoon	po hulakam	isteghindá	pas anfor-dring	på anfordring
á vista	op zight, á vista	po pradlavleni	ghiordu-ghiondo	a vista	vid sigt
á ... dias vista	dagen na sigt	po pradlavleni	ghiordu-ghinoddu sora	efter sigt	efter sigt
á ... dias dato	dagen na dato	gato	tarihinden sora	efter dato	från dato
pagam á ordem	voor my, aan de order	plat it order	emriné ver	brhag at, betale til ordre	betalas till ordre
pagarei	Ik neem aan te betalen	ia obstschul	endomayé sni veririm	jeg for-pligter mig at betale	jeg förpligtar mig att betala
com interesse	met interest	ia prasentams	faiz ila	med rento	mod ränta

B

CHAPTER XI.

OF THE RATE OF INTEREST.

THE natural fluctuations in the rate of interest charged for the use of capital or its representative, money, are determined by the same causes which influence the price of any other commodity; namely, demand and supply. If there arises an unusual demand for any commodities, in the interior of a country, or from foreign lands, the extra production cannot take place without the aid of more money, and the price of that commodity by which the others are produced rises in proportion to the demand for its assistance. As the price of money rises, so will the price of the article produced advance in proportion until the demand for it subsides, when the price of the article and the rate of interest charged for the money to produce it return to their natural points.

A high rate of interest may prove the commerce of a country to be in a most flourishing and healthy condition, and it may also prove the country to be on the verge of bankruptcy. In the autumn of 1865 we have seen the rate of interest standing very high in England, and going higher in 1866, but this was attributed to an increase in the trade generally of the country; large quantities of merchandise were shipped to America on the conclusion of the war, and this would of itself be sufficient to raise somewhat the price of capital or money.

There are many persons who maintain that bankers as a body desire to keep the rate of interest as high as possible; this view is held by the writer of an article in ʻBlackwood's Magazine' for March 1866, on ʻThe Reform of the Bank of England,' and I do not hesitate to state that such is quite erroneous. On the first consideration of such a question, it will appear to the uninitiated in banking practice that a high rate of interest will be always for the benefit of bankers; but there are undercurrents at work here. In the first place, a banker always considers himself best off when his clients are well to do, and can obtain all they want to enable them to carry on their various trades prosperously, and if possible extend them. Now, when the rate of interest is high a merchant curtails his operations unless the profits promise a corresponding augmentation, and even under such circumstances, the increased profit cannot long keep pace with the rise in the rate, as the pressure must be felt somewhere sooner or later; as a high rate of interest must be hurtful to those who are borrowers, and a large part of a banker's profits are derived from discounting bills and making advances to those who bank with him, it will stand to reason that no more money than will be sufficient to keep the accounts open will remain to the credit of the banker's clients so long as the rate continues unusually high. As the rate of interest rises, the deposits are withdrawn from the banks by all persons who understand how better to employ them, and it is unnecessary to remark that the number of persons who *do* remove their money for better investment is certainly increasing. It will thus be seen that, irrespective of the possible inconvenience which may be occasioned to the banker by having his deposits withdrawn, he may lose considerably more by the absence of the profit upon the withdrawn deposits than he gets by a higher rate of interest upon a probably diminished number of discounters. Then again, in obedience to a fixed law, as the price of the article increases, so do the bad debts increase.

A high rate of interest with any appearance of permanence is sure to fill the minds of the community more or less with alarm ; and this feeling spreads very fast, as the price of money is so much a topic of conversation in all circles, and is generally most talked about, and the greatest distrust disseminated, where the question is the least understood. The banker—who will soon be made aware of any feeling of uneasiness which may be growing in the public mind—will find it necessary at an early stage to make preparations for fortifying his position ; and the only effectual means by which this can be accomplished is by keeping a larger supply of cash upon his premises, which, as a matter of course, will occasion him a further loss ; to invest it in the most saleable securities will scarcely answer his purpose, as he runs again a further risk of being obliged to sell at the moment when there is most pressure in the market, by which he suffers the loss from a fall in the price of the securities. To pursue a system of speculating in the funds or other securities is considered discreditable to a bank ; and, therefore, unless consols, exchequer bills, &c., be purchased only for the purpose of having an interest bearing reserve, such transactions are better avoided.

In seasons of scarcity, when the rate of interest is high, the banker, in exercising increased caution, will make refusals, which in many cases will be sure to give offence; the persons refused will mention the fact to their friends, and probably state as the reasons that the banker was short of funds, which will increase the general want of confidence which then prevails, and further tend to embarrass the banker's position.

When the rate of interest is high, merchants and traders in many cases get into difficulties, and apply to the banker for assistance, stating that they have much property, but at the moment are unable to realise it. The banker makes an advance, a repetition of which is soon applied for, and, as we have seen in such innumerable instances, the banker continues to throw good money after bad, the termination of which, under the best circumstances, is an indefinite lock-up, which is among the most dangerous situations, if permitted to any extent, in which a banker can place himself.

The banker offering a high rate of interest in time of pressure is imprudent, as it gives rise to the opinion that he is short of funds, and wishes to attract them—which will probably result in more of his deposits being withdrawn.

After a panic or continued pressure in the money market has spent itself, money always becomes rapidly abundant, and the banker finds himself overrun with funds which he cannot employ, and which must remain for some time in his hands, causing him a certain loss. I need scarcely add more to prove that the idea which conceives an unnaturally high rate of interest to be beneficial to the banker is an entirely erroneous one. The permanently higher rates of interest which exist in some countries, such as Sweden, Canada, &c., prove nothing in favour of such an argument, as the financial positions of these half-developed and capitalless countries have not yet advanced to that stage when the principles of competition, demand, supply, &c., have entered the field, and been allowed to exercise that regulating influence which is necessary before the monetary affairs of a country can be said to be relatively in order.

Dr. Adam Smith says: 'The riches, and, so far as power depends upon riches, the power of every country must always be in proportion to the value of its annual produce—the fund from which all taxes must ultimately be paid. But the great object of the political economy of every country

is to increase the riches and power of that country.' Panics and frequent pressure in the money
market, causing high rates of interest, although
producing a temporary increase of a banker's profits, neither conduce to his ultimate permanent
welfare, nor 'increase the riches and power of
that country,' as the difficulty of obtaining that
commodity, by which industry is set in motion and
agriculture advanced and made more productive,
will keep a country back; throw numbers of its
people out of employ, thereby sowing the seeds of
disaffection and disorder; will cause compound loss
by all descriptions of stock, plant and other kinds
of capital deteriorating by their remaining idle
and unproductive; and will impede the progress of
science and invention, by withdrawing artisans,
mechanics, &c., from their accustomed employment,
by which the general advancement of civilisation
must be retarded.

As the fluctuations in the demand and supply of
loanable capital are more frequent than with any
other description of capital, it being the commodity by whose agency all others are exchanged,
it will be evident that industry and commerce will
be affected in all their branches by the fluctuation
in the price of loans.

There is what our first writers on political economy call the 'natural rate,' either side of which fluctuations will always take place, and are always expected to take place, and for which merchants and traders are accustomed to leave a margin in their calculations.

The unnaturally high rates which have ruled in the London market during the last three or four years, can be accounted for to a great extent by the artificial pressure which is brought to bear by the number of borrowers, who seek to obtain possession of large sums of money, not for the purpose of employing it directly in assisting in the increase of the natural productions of the earth, but for the purpose of lending it again at a higher rate, thereby giving an abnormal and artificial value to money; and, as a matter of course, the farther this system can be carried with any degree of safety and permanence, in a like degree may the price at which the use of capital can be obtained bo expected to remain unnaturally enhanced.

That part which forms so important an item in a banker's profits, should be received from his clients as much for their benefit, and more so, than for his. Setting aside the pleasantness of the banker's position, when he lends his money to a

client who cheerfully pays the rate of interest demanded, there can be no doubt whatever that
neither side is benefited so well permanently, as
when a client pays a rate of interest which the
business in which he employs it will safely bear,
and the banker can part with his money with a
conviction that he will receive it *when* due, and in
the meantime will have no occasion to supply its
place at a loss.

Mr. John Stuart Mill, 'Principles of Political
Economy,' vol. ii. p. 194, says : 'Fluctuations in the
rate of interest arise from variations either in the
demand for loans, or in the supply. The supply is
liable to variation, though less so than the demand.
The willingness to lend is greater than usual at
the commencement of a period of speculation, and
much less than usual during the revulsion which
follows. In speculative times, money-lenders, as
well as other people, are inclined to extend their
business by stretching their credit; they lend more
than usual (just as other classes of dealers and
producers employ more than usual) of capital which
does not belong to them. Accordingly, these are
the times when the rate of interest is low, though
for this, too (as we shall immediately see), there
are other causes. During the revulsion, on the

contrary, interest always rises inordinately, because, while there is a most pressing need on the
part of many persons to borrow, there is a general
disinclination to lend. This disinclination, when
at its extreme point, is called a panic. It occurs
when a succession of unexpected failures has
created in the mercantile, and sometimes also in
the non-mercantile, public a general distrust in
each other's solvency; disposing every one, not
only to refuse fresh credit, except on very onerous
terms, but to call in, if possible, all credit which
he has already given. Deposits are withdrawn
from banks; notes are returned on the issuers in
exchange for specie; bankers raise their rate of ·
discount, and withhold their customary advances;
merchants refuse to renew mercantile bills. At
such times the most calamitous consequences were
formerly experienced from the attempt of the law
to prevent more than a certain limited rate of interest from being given or taken. Persons who
could not borrow at five per cent. had to pay, not
six or seven, but ten or fifteen per cent. to compen-
sate the lender for risking the penalties of the law;
or had to sell securities or goods for ready money
at a still greater sacrifice.

    'Except at such periods, the amount of capital

disposable on loan is subject to little other variation than that which arises from the gradual process of accumulation; which process, however, in
the great commercial countries is sufficiently rapid
to account for the almost periodical recurrence of
these fits of speculation; since, when a few years
have elapsed without a crisis, and no new and
tempting channel for investment has been opened
in the meantime, there is always found to have
occurred, in those few years, so large an increase
of capital seeking investment, as to have lowered
considerably the rate of interest, whether indicated
by the prices of securities or by the rate of dis-
•count on bills; and this diminution of interest
tempts the possessors to incur hazards, in hopes of
a more considerable return.'

It will thus be seen that the rate of interest
which may be ruling at one period or another is
not influenced by the amount or value of money
which may be in circulation.

As the rate of interest rises, all descriptions of
securities become depressed; and there is always
the danger that bankers will be tempted to lend
too large a proportion of their deposits, so that
when demanded by the depositors they may be
unable to return them.

APPENDIX.

The following is copied from the 'Times' of May 18, 1866.

The return from the Bank of England for the week ending May 16, 1866, gives the following results, when compared with the previous week :—

Rest . . . £3,343,412	Increase	. .	£105,625
Public deposits . 5,936,219	„ . .	.	154,392
Other deposits . 18,620,672	„ . .	.	5,106,135

On the other side of the account :—

Government securities £10,837,056	Decrease	.	£57,198
Other securities . . 30,943,259	Increase	.	10,099,042
Notes unemployed . 730,830	Decrease	.	4,219,495

The amount of notes in circulation is 26,120,995*l*., being an increase of 3,776,600*l*. ; and the stock of bullion in both departments is 12,323,805*l*., showing a decrease of 832,335*l*. when compared with the preceding statement. *This is the most extraordinary return ever presented.* On neither of the two preceding occasions of the suspension of the Bank Act did the figures exhibit any very violent change, but in this instance the peculiar severity of the panic caused an extra 10 millions to be applied for by the public in the shape of discounts and temporary advances, of which 5,105,135*l*. found its way back in the shape of bankers' balances, and between four and five millions went into circulation in the form of remittances of notes and coin to country bankers and others. Under these circumstances, although the receipts of foreign bullion during the week exceeded the withdrawals for exportation by 93,000*l.*, the stock held shows a decrease of 832,335*l.* As the reserve of notes and bullion in the banking department still amounts to 1,202,810*l.*, it will be seen that no actual infringement of the Act has taken place, and consequently, that no Parliamentary action will be requisite.

In reply to the questions of two honourable members of the House of Commons, put to the Chancellor of the Exchequer on May 17, 1866, Mr. Gladstone, in informing them that they were under a misapprehension as to the Bank of England not having made advances ' upon the lodgment of Government securities,' stated that :—

'The advances made by the Bank of England on Government securities on Friday, the day of the panic, amounted to 919,000*l.* ; on Saturday, to 747,000*l.*, and on three subsequent days various amounts, making up the total amount advanced on these securities in five days to 2,874,000*l.* Then, with regard to the accommodation of commerce in general, the best measure that can be given of the manner in which the Bank has exercised its functions is shown in this—that it has made advances upon bills, and has discounted bills to the extent of 9,350,000*l.*, making a total of advances and discounts in five days of 12,225,000*l.*'